NEW PRACTICE READERS

THIRD EDITION

BOOK B

D1607093

DONALD G. ANDERSON

Associate Superintendent, Retired
Oakland Public Schools
Oakland, California

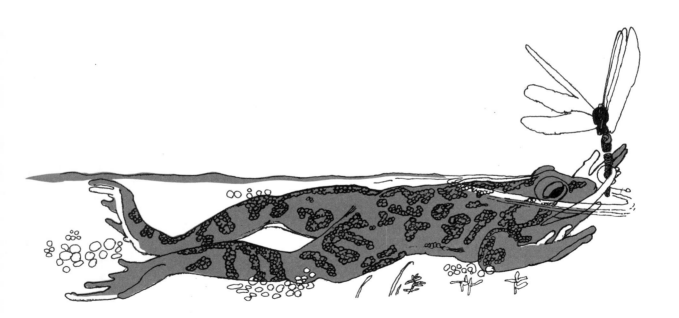

NEW PRACTICE READERS
THIRD EDITION
BOOK B

Phoenix Learning Resources
New York • St. Louis

NEW PRACTICE READERS
THIRD EDITION
BOOK B

We wish to express our appreciation for permission to adopt and use copyrighted material as follows:

For "How the Skunk Got White on His Fur" from *When Coyote Walked the Earth: Indian Tales of the Pacific Northwest* by Corinne Running. Copyright, 1949, by Corinne Running. By permission of Holt, Rinehart and Winston, Inc.

For "Why the Porcupine Cannot Shoot His Quills"
"Why Rocks Cannot Travel"
"How the Beaver Lost the Hair on His Tail"
"Why the Sun Comes Up Slowly"
from *Why the North Star Stands Still* by Wm. R. Palmer.
Copyright, 1946, 1957, permission by Wm. I. Palmer.

For "How the Animals Stole Springtime" from *Kootenai Why Stories* by Frank B. Lindeman. Copyright, 1926 Scribners. Renewal 1954, Wilder J. Lindeman, Verne B. Lindeman, and Norma L. Waller; permission by Scribner.

For "How Medicine Came to the Indians" by Amy Cruse from the *Young People's Book of Myths.* Copyright 1927 (pp. 141–145), permission by Little, Brown & Co.

Project Management and Production: Kane Publishing Services, Inc.
Cover Design: Pencil Point Studios
Text Design: Craven and Evans, Inc.
Illustrators: Shana Gregor, Lucinda McQueen, Jan Naimo, Mike Quon, William Singleton, Wayne Anthony Still

ISBN 0-7915-2118-4

5 6 7 8 9 0 05 04 03 02 01

TO THE TEACHER

This book is one of a seven-book series intended to provide reading interest and comprehension skill development for readers who need additional practice material to achieve mastery. The controlled reading level of each book makes it possible to assign students to the text most suitable for individual reading comfort.

Readabilities for this book are 2.4–3.5, consistent with the Spache Readability Formula. The reading level should be comfortable for students whose reading skills are adequate for beginning third grade.

Words not on the formula's list of familiar words were largely limited to words in use in primary basal materials. In some cases, the content required the use of challenge words. In such cases, these words appear in the readiness exercises or are supported by strong context clues in the articles themselves.

This book contains eight groups of articles in units labeled A–H. Within each unit, there are eight reading selections about factual material.

Before each article, there is a readiness activity to introduce new words. This work should be carefully supervised by the teacher before the pupils begin the article itself.

The words are defined in multiple choice or completion situations. Students must consider every word on the readiness list as they answer the preliminary questions. If this section is not handled as oral group work, pupils should have access to individual dictionaries.

Following each regular article is a test that is especially designed to improve specific skills in study reading. The charts at the end of this book may be used to record success with each skill tested. Thus, the teacher and the pupil can make a diagnosis of specific skill weaknesses as well as keep track of progress in each aspect of reading.

The skills tested are consistent with the skills tested on widely accepted reading achievement tests. At this level, the follow-up skills practiced throughout the book are:
1. Finding specific answers and giving details. In questions of this type, particular words from the article must be used to complete the sentence. Students gain practice in remembering details from their study reading. Question 1 is always of this type.
2. Recognition of implied details. Question 2 requires students to select a correct answer from among a group of three inferences. The correct answer is a reasonable conclusion (not one directly stated) drawn from ideas contained in the reading.
3. Meaning of the whole. This question requires that the student select the answer that best describes the central theme of the story.
4. and 5. Determining whether a given idea has been stated affirmatively, negatively, or not at all within the reading matter. To answer these questions, pupils need to verify that the information is correctly stated. Questions 4 and 5 give practice with this skill.
6. Recognition of the meaning of a word in context. Question 6 is this type.

At the conclusion of each unit A–G, there is a longer story prepared for recreational reading. These stories come from folktales and are intended both as pleasure reading and as a basis for group discussion. The *Thinking It Over* questions following each story may be used to launch the discussion. In certain cases, it is possible to ask students to write whole-sentence answers for additional skill development.

All the selections may be used with average or better readers to develop reading speed when desired. If a time limit is used, it should be standardized. Have all students read the first article and take the following test. Then fix the time limit based on the time taken by 90 percent of the students. For timing, use a watch or clock with a second hand. Announce, "Begin," when the second hand is at 12. Record the time in minutes and seconds. The recreational reading selections have word counts for determining speed.

Students should be urged to increase their speed only in terms of their own results.

A sample exercise follows. The directions given in color explain the procedure.

Ideally, the teacher will work through the sample exercise in some detail, directing and modeling the desired behavior. Thereafter, most pupils will be able to proceed independently.

Read-along cassettes to help the most dependent students are available for Books A, B, C, and D.

HOW TO USE THIS BOOK

There are three parts to each lesson.
1. Questions to help you get ready.
   Read them. Write the answers.

Getting Ready for the Next Story

SAY AND KNOW	Draw a line under the right word and fill in the blank.
playful	**1.** It means **a wide smile.** grin humor frown
grin	
dolphin	**2.** It has an **f** sound spelled with **ph.** bottle tease dolphin
bottle	
nosed	**3.** It means **to play jokes on.** playful learn tease
tease	**4.** Write the first small word in **playful.** _____

2. A Story to read.

Sample   A Sea Clown

In the warm waters of the sea lives a playful animal with a big grin. This animal, the bottle-nosed dolphin, is a cousin to the whale.

The dolphin likes to play around ships at sea. Even when caught and kept in a tank, it shows a sense of fun. It will tease the fish and animals around it. Dolphins love to play catch. They will throw back what they catch. They can learn many tricks. They will jump through hoops for fish.

3. Questions to tell how well you read.
   Read them. Write the answers.
   Put the number you get right in the square.

Sample   Testing Yourself   **NUMBER RIGHT**

1. The dolphin is a sea animal with a sense of _____.

   Draw a line under the right answer.

2. From the story, you can tell that
   a. a dolphin is a big whale.   b. a dolphin loves to play.

3. The story as a whole is about
   a. the whale   c. ships at sea.
   b. playing catch.   d. the bottle-nosed dolphin.

4. A dolphin swims very slowly.   Yes   No   Does not say

5. Dolphins refuse to play catch.   Yes   No   Does not say

6. What word in line six of the story means **to play jokes on?** _____

xi

Answers to Sample—A Sea Clown

Check your work. If you made a mistake,
find out why. Count the number you got
right and mark the score on your paper.

Getting Ready for the Next Story	Testing Yourself
1. grin	1. fun
2. dolphin	2. b. (a dolphin loves to play)
3. tease	3. d. (the bottle-nosed dolphin)
4. play	4. Does not say
	(Be sure to answer **Yes** only when you can find the answer in the story.)
	5. No (See sentence six)
	6. tease (This question may ask you to count lines or sentences. Be sure to do what the book asks.

Keeping Track of How You Are Doing

At the back of your book, beginning on page
144, there are record charts. Turn to the chart on
page 144 and read the directions. After you finish
each of your lessons, put your total score into the
right block on page 144.

Then turn to page 146. Read the directions
there. On pages 147 and 148, you will be keeping
track of how well you do on each type of question.
Work to improve your score.

If your teacher asks you not to mark in your
book, get help to make a copy of the record charts.

xii

NEW PRACTICE READERS

THIRD EDITION

BOOK B

Getting Ready for the Story

SAY AND KNOW

lizard

dragon

bluff

bluffer

ceiling

glass

Draw a line under the right word or fill in the blanks.

1. Does **dragon** rhyme with **wagon?**   Yes   No

2. Does **bluff** end with the same sound as **wolf?**   Yes   No

3. Write the letter you do not hear in **ceiling.** _____

4. Write the word that **bluffer** comes from. _____

A-1   Playing Tricks

Lizards are great bluffers. They can get themselves out of danger in many different ways. One lizard leaves its tail behind when something takes hold of it. Another can also blow itself up, so that it looks three times as big as it is.

The most surprising thing about these animals is the way different kinds of lizards move about. Some have legs; some do not. Some seem

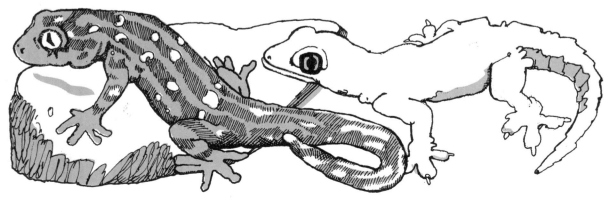

to find it easy to walk upside down on a ceiling or to hold onto glass. Some kinds can stand straight up and run on their two back feet.

There are even lizards that can swim. Others can almost fly. They jump from tree to tree. We call these lizards "flying dragons."

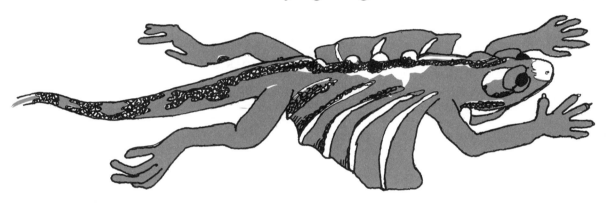

A-1 Testing Yourself   NUMBER RIGHT

1. The lizard is a big .

   Draw a line under the right answer.

2. From the story you can tell that
      a. lizards are of many sizes.   b. a lizard can get along without a tail.
                     c. lizards are usually green.

3. The story as a whole is about
      a. walking upside down.   c. many kinds of lizards.
      b. how lizards lost their tails.   d. flying lizards.

4. Some lizards can stand up and run.   Yes   No   Does not say

5. All lizards have legs.   Yes   No   Does not say

6. What word in line two of the story means **not the same?** _____

Getting Ready for the Next Story

SAY AND KNOW

termite

insect

harm

through

king

queen

worker

soldier

most

mostly

Draw a line under the right word or fill in the blanks.

1. Which word means the same as **hurt?**   harm   most   insect

2. Which word means **any of the tiny animals with three pairs of legs?**   worker   insect   through

3. Which word means **a woman who rules?**   king   queen   termite

4. Which word rhymes with **blue?**   ant   black   through

5. Write the word that **mostly** comes from. _____

6. Write the word that means **someone in the army.**

_____

A-2   The House Eaters

Termites are little insects. They are about as small as ants. They may not be large, but they can do much harm. Termites eat paper, cloth, and wood. They can eat right through a book from cover to cover. They eat chairs and tables and walls of houses, too.

Termites live in cities, or nests, the way ants do. Each nest has a king and queen and many workers and soldiers. The young kings and queens have wings for a short time. They use them only once. They fly to find a new home. Once they move in, they never fly out again.

4

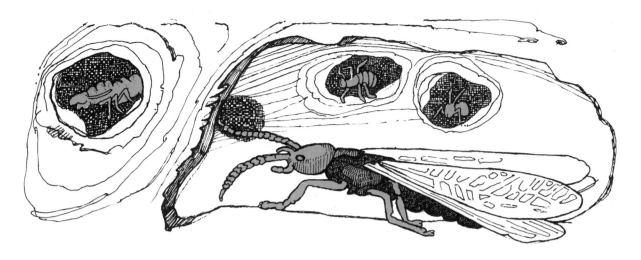

Termites are found mostly in places where it is warm. Some kinds live underground. Some kinds live in wood. No matter where they make their homes, they always do much harm.

A-2 Testing Yourself

NUMBER RIGHT

1. Termites are insects which are as small as ——————.

Draw a line under the right answer.

2. From the story you can tell that
    a. termites can live in water.   b. not all termites are harmful.
        c. termites are found mostly in warm climates.

3. The story as a whole is about
    a. insects which harm people.   c. insects which cannot fly.
    b. termites, the wood eaters.   d. how termites are like ants.

4. Soldier termites fly to find new homes.   Yes   No   Does not say

5. Some termites live underground.   Yes   No   Does not say

6. What word in line seven of the story means **large towns?** ——————

5

Getting Ready for the Next Story

web

webbed

sticky

tongue

spider

snake

croak

favorite

Draw a line under the right word or fill in the blank.

1. It is **a noise.**   web   croak   sticky

2. Paste feels like this.   **silky**   **spider**   **sticky**

3. A **webbed** foot has skin between the   **feet**   **toes**   **heels.**

4. It means **the one liked best.**   spider   tongue   favorite

5. It has only one syllable.   **sticky**   **tongue**   **croaker**

6. It is **an animal with eight legs.**   croak   snake   spider

7. Write the letter you do not hear in **croak.** _____

A-3   Croakers

Some animals live only on land, and others live only in the water. Frogs can live both on land and in water. They have webbed toes and long back legs which help them swim. On land, their strong back legs help them make long jumps.

A frog's tongue is sticky. On land or in water, the frog can catch bugs and spiders just by putting out its tongue.

6

At times, frogs can be heard calling to each other. Each kind of frog has its own call, but to us, all their calls sound like croaks.

Frogs help us by eating insects. But there are many animals which eat frogs. Snakes, birds, and fish do. People eat frogs, too. In many countries, frogs' legs are a favorite dish for dinner.

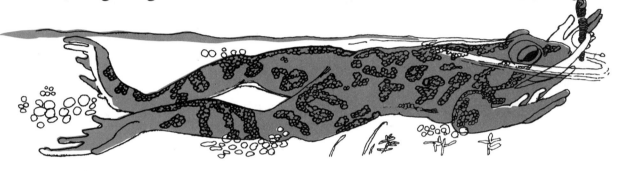

A-3 Testing Yourself

NUMBER RIGHT

1. A frog's tongue is ——————————— .

   Draw a line under the right answer.

2. From the story you can tell that
   a. frogs will die on land.   b. a frog lives on insects.
           c. frogs have few enemies.

3. This story as a whole is about
   a. frogs' legs as food.   c. how frogs swim.
   b. the frog's tongue.   d. an animal that croaks.

4. A frog's call is a croaking sound.   Yes   No   Does not say

5. A frog catches spiders with its feet.   Yes   No   Does not say

6. What word in the last line of the story means **the evening meal?** ——————

Getting Ready for the Next Story

SAY AND KNOW

strange
strangest
tales
salmon
born
die
stream
downstream
ocean
float

Draw a line under the right word or fill in the blank.

1. It means the same as **sea.**   ocean   pond   float

2. It means the same as **stories.**   tails   tales   words

3. It is **a kind of fish.**   sea   salmon   catch

4. It begins most like **stream.**   seem   strange   seen

5. It means **the opposite of born.**   come   live   die

6. It rhymes with **boat.**   bear   floor   float

7. Write the letter you do not hear in **salmon.** _____

A-4   To Sea and Home Again

One of the strangest tales of the sea is the story of the salmon. Salmon are not born in the sea at all. They are born in small, fresh-water streams.

As soon as they are born, they start a long trip downstream to the river that flows into the

ocean. In the ocean, they eat and play. They swim far, far away while they are growing. But once grown, salmon swim back to fresh water to lay their eggs.

No one knows how they find their way back through the ocean, to the rivers, and sometimes even to the little streams where they were born. But they do.

Home again, they lay their eggs. Now, the salmon are thin and tired. They float downstream to die.

A-4   Testing Yourself   **NUMBER RIGHT**

1. Salmon are born in small, fresh-water _____.

Draw a line under the right answer.

2. From the story you can tell that
    a. salmon live most of their lives in the ocean.
    b. salmon are fully grown when they reach the ocean.
    c. salmon will lay their eggs in the ocean.

3. This story tells us about
    a. fishing.   c. all the fish in the ocean.
    b. the life of the salmon.   d. fish eggs.

4. We know how salmon find their way home.   Yes   No   Does not say

5. After they lay their eggs, salmon die.   Yes   No   Does not say

6. What word in line six of the story means **with the water flow?**

_____

Getting Ready for the Next Story

SAY AND KNOW

Draw a line under the right word or fill in the blank.

trap

silk

eyepiece

telescope

microscope

different

crop

helpful

widow

1. It is used for catching animals.   **crop**   **trap**   **silk**

2. It means **not alike**.   **different**   **strange**   **spider**

3. It is used to see the stars.   **sky**   **see**   **telescope**

4. It means **useful**.   **helpful**   **widow**   **microscope**

5. It begins like **window**.   **crop**   **spider**   **widow**

6. It rhymes with **hop**.   **silk**   **crop**   **widow**

7. Write the first small word in **eyepiece**. _____

A-5   At Home in a Trap

Spiders are small animals that spin silk webs. They use their webs to trap the insects which they eat. Spiderweb silk is very strong. We use it for cross hairs in the eyepieces of telescopes and microscopes. We could use it for making clothes, if we could get enough of it. But it is hard to put spiders to work making silk for us. When many spiders are placed together, they eat each other.

Spiders eat different kinds of insects. This makes them very helpful to farmers. Some of the insects that spiders eat would do much harm to crops.

10

In this country, only a few spiders hurt people. One is a small black spider with a red spot on its underside. It is called the black widow.

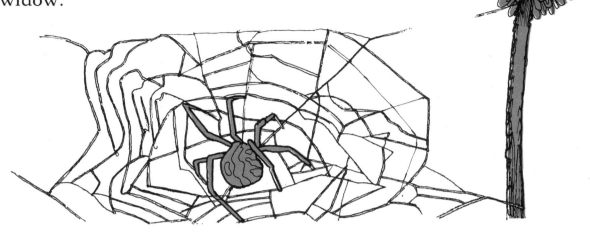

A-5 Testing Yourself

1. Spider webs are made of _____.

Draw a line under the right answer.

2. From the story you can tell that
    a. farmers do not like spiders.
    b. it is easy to get spiderweb silk.
    c. most spiders are harmless.

3. The story as a whole is about
    a. spider silk.   c. spiders that make telescopes.
    b. spiders that hurt people.   d. a small animal that spins a web.

4. Spiders use their webs to trap their food.   Yes   No   Does not say

5. The black widow spider is harmful.   Yes   No   Does not say

6. What word in line twelve of the story means about the same as **damage?**

_____

Getting Ready for the Next Story

SAY AND KNOW

flick

fin

spread

glider

far

farther

southern

coast

California

school

Draw a line under the right word or fill in the blank.

1. **A quick move of something that bends** is a

wing   flick   fly.

2. It is carried by the air. **fast   boat   glider**

3. It is **part of a fish.**   **fin   swim   sea**

4. It means **many fish swimming together.** far   fly   school

5. It has a sound like the **e** in **men.** me   meat   spread

6. It is a state in our country. **south   far   California**

7. Write the word that **southern** comes from. _____

A-6 Flying without Wings

Have you ever seen a flying fish? Some fish can come up out of the water and "fly" through the air. They can fly right over small boats!

The flying fish does not fly the way birds do, for the fish does not really have wings. The flying

12

fish throws itself from the water with a strong flick of its tail. Once in the air, it spreads its large fins. It uses these fins like the wings of a glider. The bigger the fish, the farther it can "fly." But no flying fish can stay in the air very long. It soon drops back into the water.

Flying fish live in all the warm seas. In our country, many are found off the coast of southern California. Sometimes, large schools of fish are seen, all "flying" together.

A-6 Testing Yourself

NUMBER RIGHT

1. Flying fish have no _____.

   Draw a line under the right answer.

2. From the story you can tell that
   a. flying fish can stay in the air for an hour.
   b. small fish fly the farthest.
   c. flying fish are not found in cold northern seas.

3. The story as a whole is about
   a. how flying fish fly.   c. how to catch a flying fish.
   b. how flying fish swim.   d. how wings are used.

4. Some fish fly in the same way birds do.   Yes   No   Does not say

5. Flying fish live where it is cold.   Yes   No   Does not say

6. What word in line thirteen of the story means **land along the sea?**

   _____

Getting Ready for the Next Story

crocodiles
swamps
nostril
jaws
snap
swallow
break
easy
easily
easier

Draw a line under the right word or fill in the blanks.

1. It means **wet, soft lands.**   plains   swamps   break

2. It is **the opening into a nose.**   smell   nostril   sniff

3. It starts most like **swallow.**   snap   shall   swamp

4. It is **the lower part of the face.**   webbed   jaw   snap

5. It begins like **crack.**   break   crocodile   snap

6. Write the two words that come from **easy.**

_____   _____

A-7   The Big Snap

Crocodiles are found in swamps and in slow-moving rivers of warm countries. Their feet are webbed. They can walk easily on soft, wet ground. The eyes and nostrils of the crocodile are higher than the rest of its head. Crocodiles can keep their eyes and nose above the water as they move about, looking for food.

A crocodile's mouth is large. The jaws are very strong. They can break a piece of wood in two with just one snap.

Though its mouth is big, a crocodile can swallow only small animals. When it wants to eat something big, it breaks it in two.

14

It is easier for a crocodile to close its mouth than to open it.   A strong person can hold a crocodile's mouth shut with nothing but two powerful hands!

A-7   Testing Yourself   **NUMBER RIGHT**

1. The feet of crocodiles are _____ .

Draw a line under the right answer.

2. From the story you can tell that
    a. a crocodile can live in a cold climate.
    b. a crocodile eats only small animals.
    c. a crocodile must live near water.

3. The story as a whole is about
    a. where to find a crocodile.   c. the crocodile's nostrils.
    b. an animal called the crocodile.   d. what crocodiles eat.

4. A crocodile swallows large animals whole.   Yes   No   Does not say

5. A strong person can hold a crocodile's mouth shut.
                                    Yes   No   Does not say

6. What word in line ten of the story means **a sudden bite?** _____

15

Getting Ready for the Next Story

SAY AND KNOW

crab
shallow
pincer
fighting
enemies
bend
elbow
fish
fishers
seafood

Draw a line under the right word or fill in the blanks.

1. It means **not very deep.**   splash   shallow   shell

2. It is **where your arm bends.**   neck   elbow   turn

3. It begins with the same sounds as **cry.**   try   tie   crab

4. It means **claws that can pinch.**   fish   beak   pincers

5. What word means **more than one enemy?** _____

6. What letters are silent in **fighting?** _____ _____

A-8   Safe in Its Shell

Every ocean of the world has crabs in it. Some crabs live in shallow waters, close to land. Others live in deep waters, far out at sea. But not all crabs live in the ocean. Some crabs live on land.

All crabs have legs which bend the way your arms do at the elbows. Their front legs are large with strong claws on the ends. These claws are

16

called pincers. The pincers are used for catching and killing small animals. They are also used for digging and fighting.

The crab is covered with a hard shell. This keeps it safe from some of its enemies, but not from people. All over the world, the crab is a favorite seafood. Crab fishers use large nets to catch this hard-shelled animal of the sea.

A-8 Testing Yourself

NUMBER RIGHT

1. Crabs' claws are called _____ .

Draw a line under the right answer.

2. From the story you can tell that
   a. a crab is safe from all enemies.   b. the crab's legs are jointed.
            c. crab meat is not eaten much.

3. The story as a whole is about
   a. the way crabs fight.   c. what crabs eat.
   b. the shell of the crab.   d. an animal called the crab.

4. A crab has claws.   Yes   No   Does not say

5. Crabs will sometimes fight.   Yes   No   Does not say

6. What word in line twelve of the story means **a stiff cover?** _____

Why Rocks Cannot Travel

The first time the god Shinob met a rock, he did not know what it was.

"You are too small to be a mountain," Shinob said. "Stand up and walk around. Let me take a better look at you."

But the big rock could not stand. It had no feet. It could not walk, and it could not run. It could not even roll.

So Shinob laughed at the funny thing and walked away.

The rock was angry. It knew that it was very strong, and it did not like to be laughed at.

After Shinob went away, the rock tried to move. It pushed itself, end over end, and soon it learned to roll. Every day it tried to move. At last, the rock could roll as fast as a deer can run.

One day, Shinob came by again. The rock saw the god coming, and it started to roll toward Shinob.

Shinob was afraid and began to run. But the rock kept coming closer.

Shinob ran through the woods. But the trees could not stop the rock. It rolled right over them.

Some of the animals tried to stop the rock, but the rock rolled over the animals, large and small, without even slowing down.

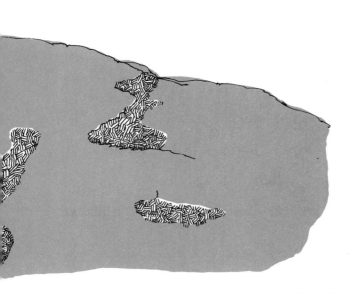

Then Shinob saw a hawk. "Help me! Help me!" Shinob cried. "I am too tired to run much more."

"I will help you," said the hawk.

The little hawk came darting down and gave the rock a peck. Then it waited until the rock turned over, and it pecked at the same spot once again.

At first, the rock laughed, for it did not even feel the pecking. But after the hawk had hit the same spot again and again, a strange feeling ran up and down inside the rock.

Now it saw that Shinob was getting away. So the rock gave a jump to catch up with Shinob. It landed on the spot where the hawk had been pecking, and *c-r-rack!* It broke in two!

Shinob was saved but was very angry. The god said, "From this day on, rocks may travel only when they are carried. When a rock falls from a mountain, it may roll as far as the bottom. There it will break into pieces and lie still."

This is how it came about that rocks cannot travel.

MY READING TIME _____ (400 WORDS)

Thinking It Over

1. Did the rock have a right to be angry because Shinob had laughed at it?

2. Did the rock have to hurt Shinob because he had laughed at it?

3. If someone makes you angry, is it right to try to hurt that person?

Getting Ready for the Next Story

beaver
lodge
dam
twigs
flat
slap
warn
builders
smartest

Draw a line under the right word or fill in the blank.

1. It is **a kind of house.**   lodge   dam   lake

2. It means **to put on guard.**   say   warn   tell

3. It has a sound like the **j** in **jump.**   pond   flat   lodge

4. It begins like **twenty.**   slap   when   twigs

5. Which word means **the most smart?**   better   beaver   smartest

6. Write the smaller word in **builders.** _____

B-1   Builders at Work

The smartest builders in the animal world
are beavers. They live in lakes and rivers, where
there are trees nearby. They cut the trees down
and eat the bark and twigs. Then they cut the
trees into pieces and build dams and homes with
them.

Beavers build their homes beside the water. A beaver's home is called a lodge. It has a sleeping room over the water and a storeroom under that.

Beavers do their woodcutting with their teeth. The teeth wear down, but they keep growing back as long as the animal lives.

Besides being very good with wood, beavers swim well, too. Their back feet are webbed. Their tails are flat. Their webbed feet and flat tails help them swim. When a beaver is afraid, it slaps the water with its tail to warn the other beavers.

B-1   Testing Yourself   **NUMBER RIGHT**

1. The beaver's house is called a _____.

   Draw a line under the right answer.

2. From the story you can tell that
   a. beavers have sharp teeth.   b. beavers eat fish.
           c. beavers do not swim.

3. The story as a whole is about
   a. what beavers eat.   c. how beavers live.
   b. how beavers swim.   d. webbed feet.

4. The beaver's tail is round.   Yes   No   Does not say

5. Beavers build dams.   Yes   No   Does not say

6. What word in line sixteen of the story means **without bumps?** _____

Getting Ready for the Next Story

SAY AND KNOW

Draw a line under the right word or fill in the blanks.

whale

1. It is **an animal.**   farm   earth   whale

breath

2. It sounds the same as **wait.**   wet   weight   white

breathe

3. It means **something that is true.**   ago   what   fact

large

largest

4. It was **an animal like a very big lizard.**

dinosaur   beaver   whale

weight

5. Write the letter you do not hear in **breath.** _____

earth

dinosaur

6. Write the word that **largest** comes from. _____

B-2   The Biggest

Did you know that the whale is like a land animal? Even though they live in the sea, whales are not fish. They breathe as land animals do. They must hold their breath under water.

The whale is the largest animal on Earth. In fact, it is the largest animal that has ever lived. Not even the great dinosaurs that lived long ago were so large as the largest whales of today.

How can any animal be so big? A land animal can have only as much weight as its legs will carry. A bird must be light so its wings can hold it in the air. But a whale does not have to stand

on its own legs. The water holds it up. So a
whale can be much bigger than a land animal.

B-2   Testing Yourself   **NUMBER RIGHT**

1. The largest animal in the world lives in the _____.

Draw a line under the right answer.

2. From the story you can tell that
   a. a whale's legs must be strong.   b. whales cannot drown.
                c. a whale is a big animal.

3. The story as a whole is about
   a. why whales can grow so large.   c. how birds fly.
   b. the largest animal in the world.   d. dinosaurs.

4. Long ago, there were animals on earth larger than the largest whale.

                                    Yes   No   Does not say

5. The whale holds itself up with its legs.   Yes   No   Does not say

6. What word in line ten of the story means **how heavy a thing is?** _____

Getting Ready for the Next Story

SAY AND KNOW

body

bodies

stomach

lungs

slow

slowly

crane

asleep

awake

whether

Draw a line under the right word or fill in the blank.

1. It is **a part of your body.**   eat   stomach   breathe

2. It means **not fast.**   clock   slow   hunt

3. It begins like **crab.**   crane   grab   lung

4. It helps you breathe.   **lung**   log   home

5. It has the sound of the **th** in **that.**   catch   whether   wet

6. It means **not asleep.**   slowly   awake   whether

7. Write the letter you drop to make the word **bodies** from

   body. _____

B-3   Good Night!

Everyone needs sleep to live.

When we sleep, we lie down. Our bodies
rest because we are not moving. Our stomachs
rest because we are not eating. Our lungs rest
because we are not breathing so fast. Our eyes

24

rest because they are not looking at anything. The work our bodies do while we are awake goes on while we sleep. But it goes on more slowly.

Animals need sleep, too. But some animals do not lie down and close their eyes, as we do.

Sometimes, it is hard to tell whether a cow is asleep or awake because we do not often see cows close their eyes.

Horses sleep standing up. Cranes not only sleep standing up, but they sleep standing on one leg!

B-3 Testing Yourself   NUMBER RIGHT

1. To live, we need to ——————.

   Draw a line under the right answer.

2. From the story you can tell that
       a. cows lie down to sleep.
       b. it is possible to sleep with the eyes open.
       c. our lungs stop working when we are asleep.

3. The story as a whole is about
       a. how living things need sleep.   c. people who sleep too much.
       b. animals which are like people.   d. animals that never sleep.

4. Some animals never go to sleep.   Yes   No   Does not say

5. A horse can sleep standing on one leg.   Yes   No   Does not say

6. What word in line five of the story means **moving air in and out?**

   ——————————

Getting Ready for the Next Story

SAY AND KNOW

shape

trunk

strong

smart

smell

hear

touch

Draw a line under each right answer or fill in the blank.

1. It ends like **cart.**   carry   smart   strong

2. **To feel with your hand** is to _____.

3. You use your nose to do this.   **call**   **has**   **smell**

4. It rhymes with **long.**   big   strong   shape

5. It begins with the same sounds as **train.**   very   trunk   touch

6. Write a three-letter word in the word **hear.** _____

B-4   Ears and Trunks

What animal is the biggest mammal that lives on land? What animal has a nose and a "hand" in the shape of a long trunk? What animal has bigger ears than any other animal? The answer to each question is the elephant!

Elephants are amazing animals. They are very strong and smart and they learn things fast. They talk with one another by making different

26

sounds, or calls. Elephants have more than 25 separate calls that mean different things.

Elephants can smell and hear very well. An elephant smells and hears things that are more than 2 miles (about 4 kilometers) away. Some sounds that elephants make are so low that people cannot hear them, but other elephants can. That's where their big ears really help!

Elephants use their trunk to touch things. An elephant can feel the shape of something. It also can tell if the object is hot or cold. Elephants learn a lot by using their trunk.

B-4 Testing Yourself

NUMBER RIGHT

1. Elephants talk to one another with 25 different _____.

Draw a line under the right answer.

2. From the story you can tell that
   a. elephants don't move well.   b. elephants have good eyes.
   c. elephants keep in contact with one another.

3. The story as a whole is about
   a. how strong elephants are.   c. how elephants walk.
   b. how elephants learn things.   d. an elephant's big ears.

4. Elephants call to one another to talk.   Yes   No   Does not say

5. All elephants look the same.   Yes   No   Does not say

6. What word in the eighth sentence means **not the same**?

_____

Getting Ready for the Next Story

wander
prey
friendly
fierce
fiercest
largest
strongest
mane
proud
kingly
beast

Draw a line under the right word or fill in the blank.

1. It sounds like **main.**   man   mane   train

2. **To be very puffed up about oneself** is **to be**
                              friendly   fierce   proud.

3. It has a sound like the **a** in **day.**   prey   dark   have

4. It means **the most wild.**   largest   fiercest   strongest

5. It means **to move about.**   mane   wander   prey

6. It means **like a king.**   friendly   kingly   fierce

7. Write the word that means **animal.** _____

B-5   The Great Cat

Baby lions are as gentle as baby cats.   Like cats, too, lions like to sleep in the daytime and wander at night.   A lioness hunts the way a cat hunts for a bird.   It will lie waiting until its prey is near.   Then it will spring.   A lioness can kill with one blow by breaking the neck of its prey.

Although baby lions are as friendly as kittens, big lions are not friendly at all.   Sometimes, a circus lion will kill the person who has trained it.

The lion is one of the strongest of wild animals.   But it is not the largest, and it is not

28

the fiercest.   The lion's large head and long mane
make it look proud and kingly.   This is why the
lion is called the "king of the beasts."

B-5   Testing Yourself   **NUMBER RIGHT**

1. In many ways, a lion is like a ———————.

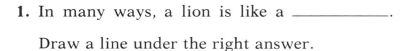

   Draw a line under the right answer.

2. From the story you can tell that
     a. a lion is not really strong.   b. the lion wanders at night.
                    c. a zoo lion is always friendly.

3. The story as a whole is about
     a. baby cats.   c. an animal that looks very proud.
     b. baby lions.   d. the fiercest animal of all.

4. The lion is a member of the cat family.   Yes   No   Does not say

5. The lion is fiercer than any other animal.   Yes   No   Does not say

6. What word in line three of the story means **chases animals?** ———————

Getting Ready for the Next Story

SAY AND KNOW

polar

walrus

seal

swimmer

dive

icy

slippery

bother

grown

Draw a line under the right word or fill in the blanks.

1. It is **a large sea animal.**   polar   walrus   fur

2. It means **near the North Pole.**   icy   bother   polar

3. It means **wet** or **icy.**   dive   slippery   slide

4. It has a sound like the **o** in **got.**   bother   mother   polar

5. It means **finished growing.**   bother   grown   dive

6. Write the letter you do not hear in **seal.** _____

7. Write the word that **swimmer** comes from. _____

B-6   At Home on the Ice

Polar bears are large, white animals that live in the icy north. They are always moving around on ice or swimming in ice-cold waters. Ice and cold do not bother the polar bears. Their heavy fur coats keep them warm, both in the water and out.

Polar bears are good swimmers. Sometimes, they swim many miles away from land. They like to dive and play in the water.

On the ice, white polar bears are very hard to see. This helps them in their hunt for food, because other animals cannot see them coming. They can move on slippery ice without sliding, for their feet are covered with fur. The fur grips the ice as they walk.

Polar bears eat walrus, fish, and seals. A full-grown polar bear may be over nine feet long.

B-6   Testing Yourself

NUMBER RIGHT

1. In the north, polar bears are hard to see because they match the _____.

Draw a line under the right answer.

2. From the story you can tell that
    a. fur soaks up water.
    b. a brown bear would find it hard to live in the icy north.
    c. polar bears sleep all winter.

3. The story as a whole is about
    a. bears.   c. what polar bears eat.
    b. the north.   d. how polar bears are suited to where they live.

4. Polar bears eat only fish.   Yes   No   Does not say

5. Polar bears keep warm by swimming.   Yes   No   Does not say

6. What word in line four of the story means **to worry?**

Getting Ready for the Next Story

SAY AND KNOW

lively
body
forests
jungles
climb
leap
few
ground

Draw a line under the right word or fill in the blank.

1. They are wild places with lots of trees. **jump jungles just**

2. It means the same as **earth** or **land**.

   ground   body   forests

3. It means **to take a big jump.** **climb   leap   use**

4. It is the main part of people or animals.

   but   body   ground

5. Which letter in the word **climb** is silent? _____

B-7   Meet the Monkey

Monkeys are smart and lively animals. They use their body to help them move around on the ground and in the trees.

Many monkeys live in forests and jungles. These monkeys have long arms and legs. They have a long tail, too. The legs, arms, and the tail of monkeys

32

help them to run, climb, and leap from tree to tree. These monkeys live in the trees most of the time.

Other monkeys live on land that has lots of grass and just a few trees. These monkeys live on the ground most of the time. But they sleep in trees.

There are different kinds of monkeys. But most monkeys eat the same things. They eat almost anything they can find! They eat birds and birds' eggs. They also eat flowers, fruit, bugs, leaves, nuts, and more.

There is a lot to know about monkeys. Find out more about them yourself.

B-7   Testing Yourself   **NUMBER RIGHT**

1. Many monkeys live in forests and _____.

   Draw a line under the right answer.

2. From the story you can tell that
   a. all monkeys live in trees.
   b. some monkeys have long arms and legs.
   c. monkeys eat special food.

3. The story as a whole is about
   a. how monkeys use their tails.   c. monkeys in trees.
   b. what monkeys are like.   d. what monkeys eat.

4. Some monkeys live mostly on the ground.   Yes   No   Does not say

5. Monkeys' bodies help them move around.   Yes   No   Does not say

6. What word in the first sentence means **full of life**?_____

Getting Ready for the Next Story

sharp
sharpshooter
spray
scent
known
shiny
stripes
bushy
enemy

Draw a line under the right word or fill in the blanks.

1. It means about the same as **shoot.**   spray   bush   stripe

2. It means **thick and spreading.**   known   bushy   fur

3. It begins like **straight.**   skunk   shoot   stripes

4. It sounds the same as **cent.**   money   change   scent

5. Write the first small word in **sharpshooter.** _____

6. What letter do you drop to make **enemies** out of **enemy?** _____

B-8   Sharpshooter

Skunks are known for their bad smell, or scent. But they are pretty little animals. Their fur is black and shiny. They have white stripes on their backs. Their bushy tails are black and white, too. They are black on top and white on the underside.

Skunks are as big as cats and make good pets. But first, they must be fixed so they cannot spray their scent.   For when they are afraid,

skunks shoot out a very bad-smelling spray. This is how they keep their enemies away. The smell stays for days and days.

The skunk often makes its home in a hole in a tree. It is more of a friend than an enemy to the farmer because it eats bugs and mice which hurt growing things.

B-8 Testing Yourself

1. The skunk is about as big as a ——————.

Draw a line under the right answer.

2. From the story you can tell that
   a. the skunk's spray is useful to the skunk.
   b. skunks are harmful to farms.
   c. skunks often live underground.

3. The story as a whole is about
   a. how the skunk protects itself.   c. where the skunk lives.
   b. how the skunk helps farmers.   d. what skunks are like.

4. When the skunk is afraid, it runs away.   Yes   No   Does not say

5. Skunks can make good pets.   Yes   No   Does not say

6. What word in line nine of the story means **to shoot a liquid?** ——————

How the Beaver Lost the Hair on Its Tail

In the long-ago time, the beaver had the most beautiful tail of any of the animals. It was wide and flat and covered all over with soft, black hair.

The beaver was a foolish animal. It was very proud of its tail. It would hold it high in the air and walk up and down for hours, showing off to the other animals.

In those far-off times, the animals did not know how to make fire. They knew that the Indians had fire. They wanted to have some, too. They had heard it was good for keeping warm, and winter was on the way.

"Let us go and see the Indians. We will give them things they like for some of their fire."

So the animals set out together for the place where the Indians lived. When they got there, they found the fire burning bright.

"How beautiful it is!" the beaver said. "And how warm!"

The animals wanted to have fire more than ever.

But, to their surprise, the people would not give up any of the fire. They wanted to keep all of it.

The animals were sad. There was nothing to do but go home. Most of them went away, but the beaver stayed behind, to show off its fine tail.

The beaver held its tail high and waved it in the air. Around and around the fire the foolish beaver went.

The people by the fire saw the beaver's tail. "That would be a fine thing to have," thought a young man. "I will catch the beaver and cut off that tail."

So the young man said to the beaver, "Come up close. Show me how you hold your tail so high."

The beaver liked to show off. It came up close, with its tail high in the air.

Swish! a hand reached out.

Just in time, the beaver saw the trick. It had to jump across the fire to get away. As it did, the beautiful tail caught on fire.

The beaver ran as fast as it could, with its tail on fire. It jumped into a nearby pond and put the fire out.

The hair on the tail was all burned off, and it never grew back. The beaver was so ashamed that it has lived close to the water, hiding its tail, from that time on.

MY READING TIME _____ **(400 WORDS)**

Thinking It Over

1. What did the beaver do that showed it was proud?

2. What did the beaver do that showed it was foolish?

3. Can you think of another animal which is said to be proud of its tail?

Adapted with permission of Prentice-Hall, Inc., Englewood Cliffs, N.J., from *Why the North Star Stands Still* by William R. Palmer. Copyright, 1946, 1957, by William R. Palmer.

Getting Ready for the Next Story

killdeer

gannet

oriole

barn swallow

saucer

fasten

branch

straw

Draw a line under the right word or fill in the blanks.

1. It means **small round stones.**   branch   pebbles   straw

2. Which bird's name is made up of two words put together?

     killdeer   gannet   oriole

3. It has the sound of the **a** in **walk.**   soup   way   saucer

4. Write the letters you must add to **fast** to make **fasten.**

   _____ _____

C-1   Anything Will Do

All birds lay eggs, and most birds build nests to hold them. Each kind of bird makes its own kind of nest.

The killdeer digs a place in the ground about as big as a saucer. It lines this with grass and little rocks.

Gannets build nests of seaweed and dirt on high rocks above the sea. Orioles fasten their nests to the ends of branches. An oriole nest is like a bag of grass and string that swings in the

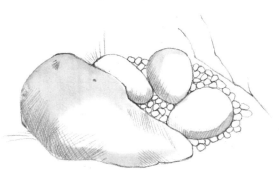

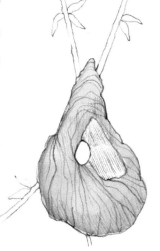

wind. A barn swallow makes a cuplike nest of mud and straw. The mother barn swallow makes the nest soft with grass and feathers.

Birds use all kinds of things for building their nests. Nests have been made of roots, hairs, egg shells, dry leaves, feathers, fur, and even the skins of snakes.

C-1 Testing Yourself   **NUMBER RIGHT**

1. Birds build nests in which to lay their _____.

   Draw a line under the right answer.

2. From the story you can tell that
   a. birds' nests are all the same size.
   b. all birds build nests.
   c. there are many different kinds of birds' nests.

3. The story as a whole is about
   a. barn swallows.   c. nests on the ground.
   b. many kinds of birds' nests.   d. snake skins.

4. All birds build their nests in trees.   Yes   No   Does not say

5. Some birds will build nests with almost anything they can find.
                                      Yes   No   Does not say

6. What word in line eight of the story means **to bind?** _____

39

Getting Ready for the Next Story

SAY AND KNOW

pigeons

squabs

popcorn

crowded

noise

human

Draw a line under the right word or fill in the blank.

1. It rhymes with **horn.**   cup   glass   corn

2. It is **a kind of bird.**   cage   pigeon   fly

3. Men and women and children are

birds   crowded   humans.

4. It has the sound of the **oy** in **boy.**   noise   bow   way

5. It begins like **crown.**   young   pair   crowded

6. It means **a sound.** _____

C-2   Pigeons and People

Pigeons like large city parks where people will feed them peanuts, popcorn, and bread. Crowded street corners, where people wait for buses and trains, are favorite spots with pigeons, too. Pigeons seem to like the smoke and noise of

40

busy places. They are not at all afraid of people. In some ways, they are even like people.

Many people think that pairs of pigeons stay together as long as they live. The pigeon father helps the pigeon mother take care of the babies. And pigeons feed their babies pigeon milk. So, you see, the pigeon family is like the human family in all these ways.

Young pigeons are called squabs. They are very good to eat. Some people raise them for food.

C-2 Testing Yourself   NUMBER RIGHT

1. Young pigeons are called _____.

   Draw a line under the right answer.

2. From the story you can tell that
   a. pigeons build nests in quiet places.
   b. pigeons can be eaten for food.
   c. pigeons are always alone.

3. This story as a whole is about
   a. what pigeons eat.   c. what pigeons are like.
   b. squabs.   d. people who raise pigeons.

4. Pigeons feed their babies a milklike juice.   Yes   No   Does not say

5. Pigeons eat insects.   Yes   No   Does not say

6. What word in line thirteen of the story means about the same as **parents**

   and children? _____

Getting Ready for the Next Story

Draw a line under the right word or fill in the blank.

solemn

wise

truth

owl

geese

crows

ravens

eyebrows

1. It means about the same as **smart**.   solemn   wise   truth

2. It means **something that is really so**.   truth   think   know

3. It has a sound like the **ou** in **loud**.   crow   owl   old

4. It means **hair above the eyes**.   nest   eyebrows   wise

5. It rhymes with **piece**.   friend   read   geese

6. Write the letter you do not hear in **solemn**. _____

C-3   How Wise, Old Bird?

An owl looks like a wise old bird. Its eyes are very large. Over them are feathers that look like heavy eyebrows. These give the owl a solemn look. It looks as if it knows more than it will tell. But the truth is that geese, crows, and ravens are all smarter than owls.

The owl cannot move its eyes from side to side. To look sideways, it must turn its head.

Even though an owl has large eyes, it does not see well in the daytime. It does its hunting at night. It helps farmers by eating rats and mice.

Owls live in trees, or in places like barns and old houses. They are not good nest builders, but they take good care of their babies.

42

C-3 Testing Yourself

1. Because of its looks, the owl is thought to be _____.

Draw a line under the right answer.

2. From the story you can tell that
    a. the owl is a wise bird.   b. farmers do not like owls.
               c. owls eat small animals.

3. The story as a whole is about
    a. geese, crows, and ravens.   c. how owls build their nests.
    b. what owls are like.   d. how owls hunt.

4. The owl is wiser than all other birds.   Yes   No   Does not say

5. Owls are good nest builders.   Yes   No   Does not say

6. What word in line three of the story means **very serious?**

_____

Getting Ready for the Next Story

SAY AND KNOW

kiwi

beak

needle

wings

shy

heavy

New Zealand

zoo

Draw a line under the right word or fill in the blanks.

1. It is **the bill of a bird.**   needle   beak   peep

2. It is **a place where animals are kept.**   fence   kiwi   zoo

3. It means **hard to carry.**   beak   earn   heavy

4. It rhymes with **things.**   **wings**   **birds**   **beaks**

5. In the word **kiwi,** both **i**'s have the sound of **e** as in **key.** Which of these words has this sound?   **shy**   **needle**   **yes**

6. Write the words that name a country.

_____   _____

C-4   A Funny Bird

"Kiwi" is the sound that a kiwi bird makes. It is a strange sound. But then, the kiwi is a strange bird. It is about the size of a hen. It has a long, thin beak, which sticks out from its head like a needle. It has wings, but it cannot

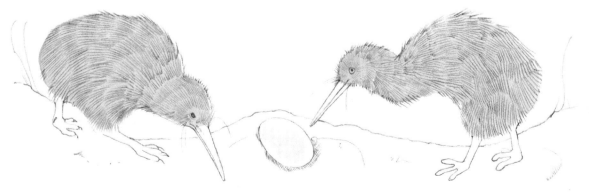

fly. It has feathers, but they do not look like feathers. They look like hair. Its eggs are so big that four of them together are as heavy as the mother bird.

Kiwi birds are very shy. They run away when people come near. They hide all day and come out only at night to hunt for food. When they sleep, they roll up into little balls.

Kiwi birds live in New Zealand, a land far away. In our country, we can see them only in zoos.

C-4 Testing Yourself 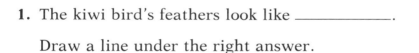 NUMBER RIGHT

1. The kiwi bird's feathers look like ⸻.

   Draw a line under the right answer.

2. From the story you can tell that
      a. the kiwi is a very small bird.   b. the kiwi likes people.
        c. the kiwi gets its name from the sound it makes.

3. This story as a whole is about
      a. what kiwi birds eat.   c. the sound that the kiwi makes.
      b. where the kiwi comes from.   d. how strange the kiwi is.

4. The kiwi can fly very fast.   Yes   No   Does not say

5. Kiwi birds have feathers.   Yes   No   Does not say

6. What word in the last sentence of the story means **places where wild animals are shown?** ⸻

Getting Ready for the Next Story

flocks

forth

arctic

tern

twenty

hours

farthest

travel

Draw a line under the right word or fill in the blanks.

1. It means **many birds together.** fly flock flew

2. It means **to go from place to place.** travel car across

3. It is **where it is very cold.** land sky arctic

4. It has a sound like the **ur** in **turkey.** hour tern twenty

5. It sounds the same as **ours.** hours south flocks

6. What word at the side means the same as **forward?** _____

7. Write the first little word in **farthest.** _____

C-5 A Great Traveler

When winter comes, great flocks of birds fly away to lands that are warm. Most birds fly many miles each year. They go back and forth to places where there is sunshine. But the bird that flies the farthest is the arctic tern.

In the summer, the arctic tern lives very near the North Pole. Here the sun shines twenty-four hours in the summer. There is no night at all. But in the fall, the tern flies south. It keeps going until it gets all the way to the South Pole. Here again, it has twenty-four hours of sunshine every day.

46

When the season changes, the arctic tern goes back to the North Pole again. The arctic tern travels thirty-five thousand two hundred kilometers (twenty-two thousand miles) every year. It is a great bird traveler.

C-5 Testing Yourself

NUMBER RIGHT

1. In the summer, the arctic tern lives near the _____ _____.

Draw a line under the right answer.

2. From the story you can tell that
    a. it is always day during the summer at the North Pole.
    b. it is always night at the South Pole.
    c. the arctic tern stays in warm countries.

3. The story as a whole is about
    a. the North Pole.   c. birds that fly south.
    b. the bird that flies the farthest.   d. how birds fly.

4. The arctic tern likes the North Pole better than the South Pole.

                              Yes   No   Does not say

5. The arctic tern flies fifty thousand miles every year.

                              Yes   No   Does not say

6. What word in line five of the story means **belonging to the North Pole?**

_____

47

Getting Ready for the Next Story

SAY AND KNOW

ostrich

camel

sandy

desert

afraid

lift

circles

Draw a line under the right word or fill in the blanks.

1. It is **a bird.**   bug   wing   ostrich

2. It is **land with no water.**   desert   ostrich   black

3. It has a hump on its back.   **beak   bird   camel**

4. It is round, like a ring.   **circle   lift   desert**

5. Something covered with sand is _____.

6. Write the word that rhymes with **made.** _____

C-6   Around and Around

The ostrich is the largest bird in the world. From far away, it looks more like a camel than a bird. It has a long neck, long legs, and a walk like a camel. Its eyes are very large and sharp. Like the camel, the ostrich can go for a long time without water. It lives in sandy deserts, too.

Its wings are too short for flying, but they do help the ostrich to run fast. The wind gets under the wings and lifts the bird off the ground. This way, it can take very long steps. An ostrich can run faster than a horse.

Ostriches are big and strong, but sometimes they do not seem very smart. When they are afraid, they run around in circles.

Ostrich eggs are large. The shells are very strong. They are so strong that they can be used for cups and bowls.

C-6 Testing Yourself

1. In some ways, the ostrich is rather like a _____.

   Draw a line under the right answer.

2. From the story you can tell that
   a. an ostrich might beat a horse in a race.
   b. ostriches need to drink lots of water.
   c. the ostrich is very clever.

3. The story as a whole is about
   a. camels.
   b. ostrich egg shells.
   c. the largest bird in the world.
   d. why an ostrich cannot fly.

4. When the ostrich is afraid, it may hide its head.   Yes   No   Does not say

5. The ostrich has wings, but cannot fly.   Yes   No   Does not say

6. What word in line nine of the story means **raises?** _____

Getting Ready for the Next Story

SAY AND KNOW

eagle
hawk
thick
hooked
tipped
bald
gold
golden
eight
prey

Draw a line under the right word or fill in the blank.

1. It means **having a bend in it.**   hawk   thick   hooked

2. It has the sound of the **a** in **face.**   bald   fast   eight

3. It is **a bird.**   eagle   bear   been

4. It rhymes with **say.**   bald   prey   toy

5. It means **the pointed end of something.**   tip   top   prey

6. It rhymes with **called.**   hooked   tipped   bald

7. Write the word that **golden** comes from. _____

C-7   Birds of Prey

Eagles are birds of prey. Hawks and owls are birds of prey, too. Birds of prey eat live animals such as squirrels, mice, and frogs. They catch these little animals with their feet.

An eagle's toes are thick and very strong. All the toes are tipped with long, hooked claws.

50

The toes and claws are used to take hold of the animals which the eagle catches and eats.

All eagles have hooked claws, and they all have large, strong bills. Still, there are many different kinds of eagles.

In our country, only two kinds of eagles are seen. They are the bald eagle and the golden eagle.

Eagles are very large birds. Their nests, too, are large. Some are as wide as two and a half meters (eight feet) across.

C-7 Testing Yourself   **NUMBER RIGHT**

1. Birds that catch live things to eat are called birds of _____.

Draw a line under the right answer.

2. From the story you can tell that
    a. the bald eagle is a very small bird.
    b. eagles are strong birds.
    c. there are many kinds of eagles in this country.

3. The story as a whole is about
    a. hawks.   c. eagles' nests.
    b. the eagle.   d. what eagles eat.

4. The bald eagle is the biggest eagle.   Yes   No   Does not say

5. Eagles' nests are larger than those of any other birds.
                            Yes   No   Does not say

6. What word in line six of the story means **having a sharp bend?** _____

Getting Ready for the Next Story

SAY AND KNOW

bright
bobwhite
goldfinch
jay
dandelion
male
female
quarrel
please

Draw a line under the right word or fill in the blanks.

1. **A man** is a   female   woman   **male**.

2. It is **a flower.**   bright   **dandelion**   goldfinch

3. It rhymes with **play.**   **jay**   gold   quarrel

4. It means **to fuss.**   talk   **quarrel**   please

5. Write the letters you do not hear in **bright.** _____ _____

6. Write the name of the color in **bobwhite.** _____

C-8 Fine Feathers

Birds' feathers help them fly, but feathers are a help to birds in other ways, too.

The color of its feathers helps a bird to hide. Some birds' feathers are brown or gray. A bob-white looks like part of the ground to an animal hunting it. It looks like old leaves or grass. Some birds' feathers are bright. A yellow goldfinch feeding on yellow dandelions in the summer is hard to see. Bright or not, their feathers help birds to hide.

Some birds have feathers that please other birds. A male's bright colors say, "Here I am!" to the female. The blue jay uses its colors in still another way. This little bird loves to quarrel with squirrels and crows and hawks. Its feathers seem to say, "See me! See me!"

C-8   Testing Yourself

1. The colors of birds' feathers help them to _____.

Draw a line under the right answer.

2. From the story you can tell that
    a. female birds have brighter colors than male birds.
    b. blue jays are hidden by their color.
    c. a bobwhite is not brightly colored.

3. The story as a whole is about
    a. how birds' feathers help them.   c. birds with bright feathers.
    b. birds with dark feathers.   d. how birds fly.

4. All birds have bright feathers.   Yes   No   Does not say

5. Only bright feathers are helpful to birds.   Yes   No   Does not say

6. What word in line fourteen of the story means **to fight with words?**

One day, the god Shinob saw a porcupine coming. The god knew that the porcupine lived alone and was afraid of everyone. So *puff!* Shinob changed into a crab.

The porcupine saw the crab. The porcupine started to run away.

"Wait!" said the crab. "Why are you afraid? You are bigger than I, but I do not run when I see you coming."

"It is easy for you to talk," said the porcupine. "You can hide inside your shell when you need to. You have claws to fight with. When you run, you run fast. But I have no shell to hide in. There is nothing on my back but hair. I have no claws to fight with, and when I run, I cannot run fast. I have no way at all to protect myself from my enemies."

"Well," said the crab, "I did not think of that." And all at once, the crab changed back to Shinob.

"Porcupine," said Shinob, "an animal should have some way to protect itself. Tell me what you want, and I will give it to you. Do

you want long, fast legs like the deer, or a shell on your back like the crab?"

The porcupine looked at Shinob. In Shinob's hand was a bow. On the god's back were arrows. "Arrows are what I want," said the porcupine. "Give me arrows, and I will not be afraid any more."

"So be it," said Shinob, putting a hand on the porcupine's back. The porcupine had a funny feeling. It looked around. Its back was covered with pointed quills, which were just like the god's arrows.

The animals of the woods came to look. They laughed at the funny-looking porcupine.

The porcupine was angry. "I will teach you not to laugh at me." With a shake, it sent its arrows flying out to hurt the other animals.

The god saw what the porcupine did. "This is bad," Shinob said. "I gave you arrows to protect you, not to hurt those who have not hurt you."

Shinob put a hand on the porcupine's back again. "From now on, you cannot throw your arrows," said Shinob. "The arrows will stick into anyone who touches you. They will protect you from your enemies. But you cannot start fights."

From that day on, the porcupine has not been able to shoot its quills.

MY READING TIME _____ (400 WORDS)

Thinking It Over

1. Why did Shinob give quills to the porcupine?

2. Why did Shinob take back the porcupine's power to shoot them?

3. Do you think it is wrong for one wild animal to hurt another because it is angry?

Getting Ready for the Next Story

SAY AND KNOW

against
gentle
breeze
hurricane
rises
rushing
stronger

Draw a line under the right word.

1. It means **moving fast.**   catching   rushing   blowing

2. It has the sound of the **e** in **ten.**   been   she   against

3. It has the sound of the **s** in **those.**   rush   rise   such

4. It means **slow and easy.**   stronger   gentle   faster

5. It means **a wind storm.**   hurricane   rushes   air

D-1   The Air Around You

You cannot see the wind, but you know
when the wind is blowing. You can feel it against
your face. You can see the leaves on the trees
moving as the wind blows them.

Wind is air that is moving. The faster the
air moves, the stronger the wind is. A gentle,

56

slow-moving wind is called a breeze. A hurricane
is a wind that is moving very, very fast.

Air moves because some air is warm and
other air is cold. When air is warm, it goes up.
When air is cold, it goes down. When the warm
air rises from the ground, the cold air nearby
rushes in to fill its place. This rushing motion
of the air is what we call wind.

D-1 Testing Yourself   **NUMBER RIGHT**

---

1. The wind that moves very fast is called **a** _____.

Draw a line under the right answer.

2. From the story you can tell that
     a. you can see wind.   b. wind stirs up the air.
         c. there would be no wind if all air were cold.

3. The story as a whole is about
     a. breezes and hurricanes.   c. how to tell when wind is blowing.
     b. air moving to make wind.   d. how leaves blow.

4. You know wind is blowing by things it moves.   Yes   No   Does not say

5. Warm air moves up, and cold air moves down.   Yes   No   Does not say

6. What word in line thirteen of the story means **moves fast?** _____

57

Getting Ready for the Next Story

hail

freeze

freezing

whole

warmer

carry

carried

carrying

Draw a line under the right word or fill in the blanks.

1. When water freezes, it turns into **rivers   rain   ice.**

2. It rhymes with **keys.   warm   freeze   carry**

3. It means **more warm.   farmer   cooler   warmer**

4. It sounds like **hole.   hail   whole   fall**

5. Write the letter you do not hear in **hail.** _____

6. Write the word from which **carried** and **carrying** come.

_____

D-2   Ice from a Summer Sky

Sometimes, during summer storms, the sky rains balls of ice. This is hail. It is made when the air near the ground is hot.

A few miles up, the air may be cold enough to freeze water. Hot air carrying water with it rises from the ground. As it pushes up into the

58

freezing air, the water freezes into drops of ice. Then this ice starts to fall down into warmer air.

As the ice falls, it passes through more water-filled air. The water makes another icy coat on each falling drop of ice. Sometimes, the wind pushes the icy drops back up into the freezing air. Then, as they come down again, they get more coats of ice.

This whole thing happens over and over again. Each time, the ice balls get bigger and bigger. They can get as big as baseballs. When the balls get too heavy for the wind, they fall as hail.

D-2 Testing Yourself   NUMBER RIGHT

1. Hail can fall during the _____.

   Draw a line under the right answer.

2. From the story you can tell that
   a. air can freeze.   b. some water is carried by the air.
   c. it cannot hail in hot weather.

3. The story as a whole is about
   a. how hot air rises.   c. how hail is formed.
   b. how heavy hailstones are.   d. how cold it gets in summer.

4. Hail never falls in the winter.   Yes   No   Does not say

5. There are many coats of ice on a hailstone.   Yes   No   Does not say

6. What word in line five of the story means **to turn into ice**? _____

Getting Ready for the Next Story

clouds

dust

weather

fluffy

thick

sunshine

changes

shapes

billions

Draw a line under the right word or fill in the blank.

1. It means **not thin.**   changes   little   **thick**

2. It means **the forms of things.**   changes   **shapes**   dark

3. It means **soft and light.**   **fluffy**   thick   pink

4. It is **fine, dry earth.**   busy   **dust**   clouds

5. It begins like **went.**   **weather**   sunshine   dust

6. What word on the left means **a very, very large number?**

_____

D-3   Color in the Clouds

Sometimes, the sky is full of fluffy white clouds. But sometimes, clouds look black. Sometimes, they look pink. Where does the color come from?

Clouds are made of drops of water or ice. But the drops of water in the clouds are not pink or red or orange. It is the sun that makes the colors in the clouds. Sunshine changes color as it goes through the drops of water in the clouds.

Clouds look dark because they are so thick. Billions of drops of water make a cloud. Very little sunshine can come through. Dust also

60

makes clouds dark.   Dust from the ground blows
into the sky and becomes part of the clouds.

The shapes and colors of the clouds tell
about the weather.

D-3   Testing Yourself **NUMBER RIGHT**

1. Dark clouds are very _____.

Draw a line under the right answer.

2. From the story you can tell that
   a. clouds are mostly water.
   b. clouds can be seen only when the sun shines through them.
   c. clouds of different shapes have different colors.

3. This story as a whole is about
   a. why clouds are black.   c. what clouds are made of.
   b. why clouds are pink.   d. why clouds seem to be colored.

4. All clouds have water or ice in them.   Yes   No   Does not say

5. Water and ice in the clouds may be pink or red or orange.
                                          Yes   No   Does not say

6. What word in line one of the story means **soft and downy?** _____

Getting Ready for the Next Story

SAY AND KNOW

sunlight

opposite

bend

bent

broken

raindrops

violet

between

Draw a line under the right word or fill in the blanks.

1. **Raindrops** are made of   **air**   **water**   **sky.**

2. It means **facing.**   **opposite**   **violet**   **mixed**

3. It means **did bend.**   **broken**   **beam**   **bent**

4. It begins like **brown.**   **down**   **broken**   **round**

5. Write the first little word in **between.** _____

6. Write the last little word in **sunlight.** _____

D-4   Now You See Them, Now You Don't

Sunlight is made of red, orange, yellow, green, blue, and violet. The colors are always there when the sun shines, but we cannot see them most of the time. When they are all together, we see white light.

When sunlight goes through water, the light rays are bent. As each ray passes through a rain-

62

drop, it breaks up into the different colors. Then we can see red, orange, yellow, green, blue, violet, and many colors in between.

After it rains, the air is full of raindrops. When the sun comes out and begins to shine, the sunbeams hit these drops. The sunlight is bent, and we see the colors of a rainbow in the sky.

Next time a rain is over, stand with your back to the sun. Look at the opposite side of the sky, and you may see a rainbow.

D-4   Testing Yourself   NUMBER RIGHT

1. A rainbow is made by the sun shining through _____.

   Draw a line under the right answer.

2. From the story you can tell that
     a. rays of sunshine are crooked.
     b. rainbows are made by sunshine and water.
     c. you can always see many colors in sunlight.

3. The story as a whole is about
     a. why sunlight has no color.   c. how color is made.
     b. how rainbows are made.   d. how rain is made.

4. Sunlight is only white.   Yes   No   Does not say

5. To see a rainbow, look away from the sun.   Yes   No   Does not say

6. What word in the last line of the story means **a bend of colors in the sky?**

Getting Ready for the Next Story

hurricanes

damage

sunsets

direction

usual

warning

weather

reporters

satellites

Draw a line under the right word or fill in the blank.

1. **Damage** can be caused by   fire   warning   direction.

2. It has a sound like the **u** in **use**.   usual   sunsets   hurricanes

3. It begins with the same sounds as **war**.

   weather   warning   usual

4. **A satellite** is most like   **an airplane**   **a boat**   **a car**.

5. It comes at the end of the day.   **morning**   **sunset**   **noon**

6. Big wind storms are _____.

D-5   Time Before the Hurricane

People living near the sea have to know when hurricanes are coming. Hurricanes are great storms with very strong winds. These winds move at one hundred twenty kilometers (seventy-five miles) an hour. They can do great damage. Sometimes, they blow boats out of the water. Houses have even been blown down.

People look for signs to tell when a hurricane may be coming. They watch for very red sunsets. They notice a change in the wind's direction. One very good sign is when the waves coming to shore come less often but are larger than usual.

64

But the best warning today comes from weather reporters. They look at pictures of the clouds taken from satellites flying high in the sky. People now have lots of time to get ready before the hurricane comes.

D-5 Testing Yourself   **NUMBER RIGHT**

1. Satellites fly in the _____.

Draw a line under the right answer.

2. From the story you can tell that
   a. hurricane winds blow in a straight line.
   b. hurricanes are storms that start over the sea.
   c. hurricane winds always blow boats out of the water.

3. The story as a whole is about
   a. satellites.   c. hurricane damage.
   b. weather reporters.   d. warnings of hurricanes.

4. Hurricane winds are strongest in the middle of the storm.

                    Yes   No   Does not say

5. A very red sunset may mean a hurricane is coming.

                    Yes   No   Does not say

6. What word in line six of the story means **harm** or **injury?** _____

Getting Ready for the Next Story

Draw a line under the right word or fill in the blanks.

tornado

windstorm

sweep

vacuum

cleaner

elephant

shelter

underground

probably

1. It means **a safe place.**   shape   shelter   hide

2. It is **a kind of windstorm.**   tornado   elephant   cleaner

3. It means **more than likely.**   wish   vacuum   probably

4. It is used for cleaning house.

   underground   vacuum cleaner   sweep

5. It means **to clean with a broom.**   sweep   shelter   whirl

6. Write the two words that make **windstorm.** _____

   _____

D-6   Clean Sweep

A tornado is a windstorm so strong that no one has been able to tell just how fast the winds blow. Some of the winds may go about four hundred eighty kilometers (three hundred miles) an hour.

The tornado is probably stronger than any other storm, even a hurricane. It is so strong, it can pull trees out by their roots. Like a great big

vacuum cleaner, it can pick up houses and trains and cars. Tornadoes sometimes blow away whole towns.

Tornado winds move very fast, but they do not last very long. As they move, they whirl the way hurricanes do. From far away, a tornado looks like a long, thick, black elephant's trunk from the sky to the ground.

People who live where tornadoes come build shelters under their houses. They hide in these underground shelters when they see a tornado coming.

D-6   Testing Yourself   NUMBER RIGHT

1. The strongest storm we know is probably the _____.

   Draw a line under the right answer.

2. From the story you can tell that
   a. a tornado is just like a hurricane.
   b. an underground shelter can protect you in a tornado.
   c. a tornado blows in a very wide circle.

3. The story as a whole is about
   a. how fast a tornado travels.   c. hurricanes.
   b. the strongest storm.   d. storm shelters.

4. A tornado is a strong, whirling windstorm.   Yes   No   Does not say

5. A tornado has the shape of an elephant.   Yes   No   Does not say

6. What word in line six of the story means **very likely?** _____

Getting Ready for the Next Story

SAY AND KNOW

thunder

lightning

explode

explosion

shot

crash

roar

slowly

mile

Draw a line under the right word or fill in the blanks.

1. It means **not fast.**   roar   mile   slowly

2. It is **a loud sound.**   **flash**   **crash**   **shake**

3. You may see it in a storm.   **thunder**   **lightning**   **explode**

4. It has a sound like the **sh** in **sheep.**   **shot**   **roar**   **though**

5. Write the letters you do not hear in **lightning.** _____ _____

6. Write the word that **explosion** comes from.

_____

D-7   Big Noise

You cannot see thunder, but you can hear it. It has the sound of an explosion, like a shot from a gun. Many people are afraid of thunder. But thunder cannot hurt you. It is only air rushing away from the heat of lightning that makes the noise.

Thunder has different sounds. Sometimes, it roars. Sometimes, it claps. Sometimes, it crashes.

Thunder and lightning always go together. It is the lightning that causes thunder. But light moves faster than sound, so you see lightning before you hear thunder.

Next time you see lightning, start to count slowly. If you count to five before you hear the thunder, you know the lightning was over one and a half kilometers (about one mile) away. If you count as far as ten, you know the lightning was about three kilometers (about two miles) away.

D-7   Testing Yourself   **NUMBER RIGHT**

1. Light travels faster than _____.

Draw a line under the right answer.

2. From the story you can tell that
    a. lightning cannot harm you.   b. lightning is carried by thunder.
          c. lightning is often far away.

3. The story as a whole is about
    a. thunder and lightning.   c. how fast thunder travels.
    b. magic.   d. things people fear.

4. We always see lightning and hear thunder at the same moment.
                        Yes   No   Does not say

5. Thunder can hurt people.   Yes   No   Does not say

6. What word in line two of the story means **a blowup?** _____

Getting Ready for the Next Story

season

summer

winter

autumn

Earth

slant

toward

month

Draw a line under the right word or fill in the blanks.

1. Summer and **winter** are   days   seasons   years.

2. A year has twelve   **summers**   **winters**   **months.**

3. We live on the   **North Pole**   **Earth**   whole.

4. It means **in the direction of.**   away   under   toward

5. To slant means to be   uneven   straight   tipped.

6. Write another name for **fall.** _____

7. Write the first little word in **toward.** _____

D-8   Tilt and Turn

Summer is warm, and winter is cold. Do you know why?

Earth moves around the sun. It is tipped on one side. Our part of the Earth has winter when the North Pole slants away from the sun. Our part of the Earth has summer when the North Pole slants toward the sun.

It takes one year for the Earth to go all the way around the sun. The sun shines on the North Pole for three months, and we have summer. Then the North Pole begins to face out from the sun, and we have autumn. When the sun is not

70

shining on the North Pole at all, we have winter. Winter turns to spring when the North Pole again faces toward the sun. Each season is about three months long.

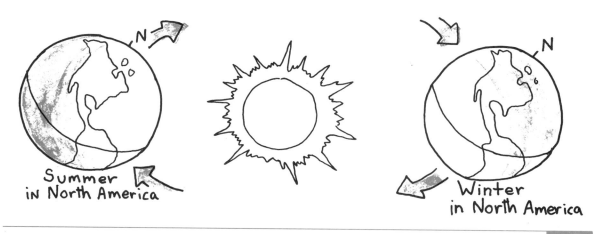

D-8 Testing Yourself **NUMBER RIGHT**

1. Each season lasts for about _____ _____.

Draw a line under the right answer.

2. From the story you can tell that
    a. seasons are caused by the way the sun shines on the Earth.
    b. the Earth moves around the sun once in three months.
    c. the sun moves around the Earth.

3. The story as a whole is about
    a. the sun.   c. the Earth.
    b. why seasons change.   d. the North Pole.

4. The Earth moves around the sun.   Yes No Does not say

5. The Earth is tipped on one side.   Yes No Does not say

6. What word in line three of the story means **slanted**?

_____

How the Skunk Got White on Its Fur

There was a time, long ago, when the skunk was black all over. It did not have white on its back. It did not have white on its tail. Other animals were afraid of it, for its scent could kill.

One winter, the wolf came to see the skunk. The wolf stayed for days and days. Soon all the food that the skunk had saved for winter was gone.

"All of my food is gone," said the skunk. "We will have to go out hunting."

"I know how to get food without going hunting," said the wolf. "I will put white dust on you to make you look pale and sick. Then I will call the other animals to come and see you. When they come, shoot them with your scent. They will fall down dead, and we will not need to go hunting."

"This is a good plan," the skunk said. So the wolf made the skunk white and went to call the goat.

"Come at once," the wolf said. "Skunk is sick and wants to see you."

They found the skunk on the ground, moaning and groaning.

"Oh, my!" said the goat. "The skunk does look sick! It is pale and white all over." Then the goat was not afraid of the skunk and ran to look closer.

Up jumped the skunk and shot the goat. The goat fell down dead.

"This is better than hunting!" said the skunk. "Go get someone else."

So the wolf went away, and the skunk lay down again. It closed its eyes and started moaning and groaning.

Now it happened that the great deer had been watching from the bushes. When the skunk lay down and closed its eyes, the deer ran over and picked up the skunk on its horns.

"I am going to kill you, Skunk!" said the deer. "I will throw you down from the mountain."

"No! No!" cried the skunk. "Let me go! I will do whatever you say."

"Will you promise never, never again to use your scent to kill?"

The deer shook the skunk so hard that the white dust flew off in a great cloud.

"Yes, I promise," said the skunk. "Put me down."

So the deer put down the skunk and let it go. From that day, the skunk has never used its scent to kill. And on its back and tail, some white has stayed to remind the skunk of its promise.

MY READING TIME _____ (400 WORDS)

Thinking It Over

1. Was it right for the wolf to plan to kill other animals?

2. Was it right for the skunk to kill the goat?

3. Was it right for the deer to say it would kill the skunk?

Adapted from "How the Skunk Got White on His Fur" from *When Coyote Walked the Earth: Indian Tales of the Pacific Northwest* by Corinne Running. Copyright, 1949, by Corinne Running. By permission of Holt, Rinehart and Winston, Inc.

Getting Ready for the Next Story

SAY AND KNOW

crack
layers
grooves
openings
caves
empire
New Mexico

Draw a line under the right word or fill in the blanks.

1. **A narrow opening in a rock** is **a   crack   lake   cave.**

2. It is **the opposite of closing.   opening   layers   empire**

3. It means **ruts** or **channels.   layers   grooves   state**

4. Write the **state** name from the list.

_____ _____

E-1   Underground Surprises

When it rains, water goes down into the ground. Some of the water feeds plants. Some runs off to fill lakes and rivers. Some finds its way deep under the ground, down to where there are layers of rock.

74

The water runs through cracks in this rock. It wears the softest rock away, and the cracks get bigger. The cracks become deep grooves. The grooves get bigger year by year and become large openings. Sometimes, the open places become as large as rooms. These great openings under the ground are what we call caves. Not all caves are made this way, but many are.

One of the largest caves in the world is in the state of New Mexico. It is so deep that the Empire State Building could lie in it.

E-1   Testing Yourself   **NUMBER RIGHT**

1. Some underground openings are as large as _____.

Draw a line under the right answer.

2. From the story you can tell that
   a. all caves are about the size of rooms in a house.
   b. it takes a long time for water to make a cave.
   c. caves are formed by water washing away dirt.

3. The story as a whole is about
   a. rain.   c. cracks in rocks.
   b. a very large cave.   d. how caves are made.

4. Water can wear away rocks.   Yes   No   Does not say

5. The Empire State Building is in New York.   Yes   No   Does not say

6. What word in line two of the story means **gives food to?** _____

Getting Ready for the Next Story

SAY AND KNOW

volcano

lava

melted

steam

gases

mountain

change

changing

Draw a line under the right word or fill in the blanks.

1. It begins like **very**.   lava   gases   volcano

2. It means **changed to liquid**.   gases   melted   rock

3. It means **melted rock**.   lava   volcano   changing

4. It is **a very high hill**.   earth   mountain   steam

5. Write the letter you do not hear in **steam**. _____

6. Write the word from which **changing** comes. _____

E-2   Fireworks

Have you ever seen hot, melted rock, steam, and gases shoot into the air from an opening deep in the ground?   A fire hole like this is called a volcano.   Volcanoes can become high mountains.

The hot, melted rock from volcanoes is called lava.   It looks like hot, steaming mud. Sometimes, a volcano will blow the lava high into the air.   Sometimes, the lava will just bubble out like stuff from a pot boiling over.

How does a volcano begin?   The earth we live on is changing all the time.   Sometimes, as the earth changes, deep cracks open into underground pockets of melted rock.   Then hot lava and

76

gases burst out. After the lava comes out, the rock cools and gets hard. Later, more lava is blown out. It hardens on the first layer. As this lava piles up, it makes a cone-shaped mountain.

E-2 Testing Yourself   **NUMBER RIGHT**

1. Rock shooting up from a volcano is so hot it is ——————.

Draw a line under the right answer.

2. From the story you can tell that
    a. volcanic rock grows in fields.
    b. volcanoes are always openings in mountains.
    c. mountains can be built up by melted rock coming out of volcanoes.

3. The story as a whole is about
    a. volcanoes.   c. the earth we live on.
    b. how high volcanoes are.   d. hot mud.

4. Lava is hot.   Yes   No   Does not say

5. Nothing changes inside the earth.   Yes   No   Does not say

6. What word in line thirteen of the story means **hollow places?** ——————

Getting Ready for the Next Story

SAY AND KNOW	Draw a line under the right word or fill in the blanks.

SAY AND KNOW

south

pole

globe

Henson

explorer

exact

Peary

Draw a line under the right word or fill in the blanks.

1. It is round like a ball. **pole   globe   box**

2. **A person who looks for new lands** is called **an**
   engineer   artist   explorer.

3. It means **just right.** **exact   pole   matter**

4. It means **opposite the North Pole.** **south   east   west**

5. It rhymes with **roll.** **pole   explorer   south**

6. Write the two words in **Henson.** _____ _____

E-3   Only One Way to Go

The North Pole is farther north than any
other place on Earth. It is easy to find on a globe.
It is where all the north and south lines come
together at the top.

If you were standing on the North Pole,
there would be only one way to go. No matter

which way you turned, you would be going south. No place on Earth is north of the North Pole.

Even though it is called the North Pole, there is really no pole there. There is not even any land. Only thick ice covers the sea. It took many years to find the exact spot where the North Pole is. The first person to reach it was a black man, Matthew A. Henson. He was with a group of explorers headed by Robert E. Peary.

E-3 Testing Yourself   **NUMBER RIGHT**

1. The farthest north you can go on the Earth is to the _____

_____.

Draw a line under the right answer.

2. From the story you can tell that
    a. the sea at the North Pole is covered with ice.
    b. it was easy to find the North Pole.
    c. no people live at the North Pole.

3. The story as a whole is about
    a. great sheets of ice.   c. the explorer who found the North Pole.
    b. the globe.   d. the place that is farthest north.

4. The North Pole is part land.   Yes   No   Does not say

5. At the North Pole, there is a pole of ice.   Yes   No   Does not say

6. What word in line one of the story means **a longer way?**

_____

Getting Ready for the Next Story

Egypt
desert
sphinx
statue
huge
block
thousands
famous
ruled

Draw a line under the right word or fill in the blanks.

1. It is **a country.**   desert   **Egypt**   huge

2. It has a sound like the **oe** in **shoe.**   toe   does   ruled

3. It means **a solid piece of something.**   huge   full   **block**

4. It rhymes with **stinks.**   desert   **sphinx**   thousands

5. Write the letter you do not hear in **statue.** _____

6. Write the word that means **well known.** _____

E-4   Ruler in the Desert

In the desert of Egypt stands a huge statue
made of stone. It is many thousands of years old.
It is almost as tall as a six-story building. It is
almost as long as a city block. It is called the
Great Sphinx.

80

This strange statue has the head of a person and the body of a lion. The head and body are cut out of rock. The paws and legs are of huge stone blocks. It is thought that the head looks like the ruler of Egypt at the time that the statue was made. No one knows which ruler it was, because it was so long ago.

The people in Egypt made many sphinxes. But the Great Sphinx is one of the most famous statues in the world.

E-4 Testing Yourself

NUMBER RIGHT

1. A sphinx is a stone —————————————.

Draw a line under the right answer.

2. From the story you can tell that
    a. the Great Sphinx is the only sphinx statue.
    b. to build the Great Sphinx must have been difficult.
    c. it took thousands of years to build the Great Sphinx.

3. The story as a whole is about
    a. stone statues.   c. a statue of a famous person.
    b. a famous statue in Egypt.   d. a statue of a lion.

4. The Great Sphinx is thousands of years old.   Yes   No   Does not say

5. There are many Great Sphinxes.   Yes   No   Does not say

6. What word in line ten of the story means **a person who governs**?

————————————

Getting Ready for the Next Story

moon

ocean

tide

reflecting

mirror

closer

travels

rockets

Draw a line under the right word or fill in the blank.

1. **The rising and falling of the ocean** is called **a**

                                                 sea   tide   water.

2. It means **nearer.**   closer   mirror   ocean

3. We see it in the sky.   moon   Earth   tides

4. It has a sound like the **o** in **move.**   cook   moon   door

5. It rhymes with **pockets.**   travels   closer   rockets

6. Write the word that means **shining back.**

_____

E-5 Mirror in the Sky

The moon is closer to the Earth than to the sun. It is closer to the Earth than to the stars. It travels around the Earth as the Earth travels around the sun. The moving of the moon around the Earth is what makes the tides in our oceans go in and out.

The full moon shines like a bright ball in the sky. But the moon does not give off any light of its own. It shines by reflecting the light it gets from the sun. If you hold up a mirror to the sun, the mirror catches the sunlight and shines. This is the way the moon shines.

For a long time, we felt sure there were no living things on the moon. Then we sent explorers up in rockets. We found it true that nothing lives there.

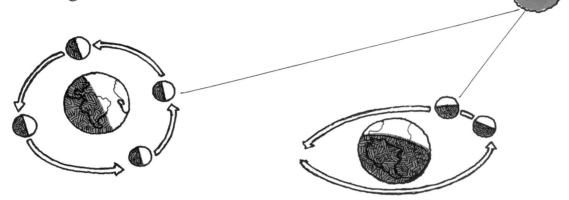

E-5 Testing Yourself

NUMBER RIGHT

1. The moon travels around the _____.

   Draw a line under the right answer.

2. From the story you can tell that
   a. the moon is not a star.   b. there are living things on the moon.
        c. the sun reflects the light of the moon.

3. The story as a whole is about
   a. the sun.   c. the Earth.
   b. the tides.   d. the moon.

4. The moving of the moon makes the tides in the seas go in and out.
                                Yes   No   Does not say

5. The moon gives off its own light.   Yes   No   Does not say

6. What word in line seven of the story means **sends off light?**

   _____

Getting Ready for the Next Story

sail

sailor

sailing

ships

canoes

brave

wonderful

someday

Draw a line under the right word or fill in the blanks.

1. They are like **boats.**   oceans   sails   ships

2. It is **a light open boat.**   ship   canoe   tanker

3. It means **very exciting.**   someday   wonderful   canoe

4. Write the letter you do not hear in **sail.** _____

5. Write the word that means **one who sails.** _____

6. Write the four-letter word in **someday.** _____

E-6   A Good Road

The ocean is like a road from one land to another.

We can use it as a road because we know how to make and use boats. Great ships carry people and goods. Goods from other countries come to us across the seas. We can buy these goods and enjoy them.

84

Long ago, people were afraid to take their small boats out onto the open ocean. It took brave sailors to be the first to sail out of sight of land.

Think of the people who took canoes and sailing ships across the oceans to unknown lands. Can you name any of these explorers? There are many wonderful stories about the great sailors of the world. Someday, you will read these stories and learn about the people who first traveled the ocean roads.

E-6   Testing Yourself   NUMBER RIGHT

1. People can travel on the ocean because they can build _____.

Draw a line under the right answer.

2. From the story you can tell that
    a. long ago, people sailed within sight of the shore.
    b. people can only fly over the ocean.
    c. people have sailed the open ocean since the first boats were made.

3. The story as a whole is about
    a. sailing.   c. goods from across the ocean.
    b. brave sailors.   d. ships on the ocean road.

4. Everything we buy crosses the ocean.   Yes   No   Does not say

5. People are still afraid to sail the ocean.   Yes   No   Does not say

6. What word in line five of the story means **things to sell?** _____

Getting Ready for the Next Story

China

valley

brick

enemy

enemies

defense

tower

inch

Draw a line under the right word or fill in the blank.

1. It is **a country.**   earth   **China**   tower

2. It means **to protect.**   **defense**   enemies   inch

3. It is **a low place between hills.**   wall   inch   **valley**

4. It is **a block of clay baked by sun or fire.**

    brick   inch   China

5. It has a sound like the **c** in **dance.**   **defense**   brick   China

6. Write the word from which **enemies** comes. _____

E-7   The Great Wall

In the country of China, there is a wall that is two thousand four hundred kilometers (one thousand five hundred miles) long. It is called the Great Wall of China. It winds uphill and down, through valleys and mountains. Every bit of this two thousand four hundred-kilometer (one thousand five hundred-mile) wall was built by hand.

The Great Wall of China was built many, many years ago. The people of China made it to keep out their enemies. There are watchtowers all along the way. The wall is built of bricks and earth. It is high and wide on top. People can walk along the top as if it were a road.

86

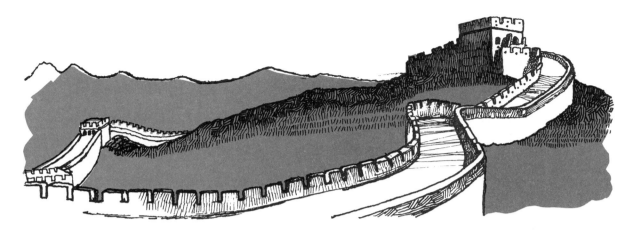

It is said that it took ten years to build just one part of this wall. No other defense line has ever been made as long as the Great Wall of China.

NUMBER RIGHT

1. The Great Wall of China is ———————————— miles long.

Draw a line under the right answer.

2. From the story you can tell that
 a. soldiers probably kept guard on the Great Wall.
 b. the Great Wall was built to be a road for carts.
 c. the Great Wall was built in a short time.

3. The story as a whole is about
 a. the longest defense line in the world. c. the people of China.
 b. the highest wall in the world. d. the roads in China.

4. The Great Wall of China is made of wood. Yes No Does not say

5. Big machines helped build the Great Wall. Yes No Does not say

6. What word in line four of the story means **moves this way and that?**

———————————

Getting Ready for the Next Story

quake	Draw a line under the right word or fill in the blank.

quake

earthquake

worst

damage

split

surface

knocked

forces

Draw a line under the right word or fill in the blank.

1. It means the same as **shake.**   quake   split   against

2. It means about the same as **top.**   tap   surface   forces

3. It is **the opposite of best.**   ten   split   worst

4. It has a sound like the **ur** in **hurt.**   use   forces   worst

5. It means **hurt.**   surface   damage   earthquake

6. It means **hit.**   knocked   strong   worst

7. Write the four-letter word which ends **surface.** _____

E-8   Earthquakes

One of the worst things that can happen on our earth is an earthquake. When earthquakes happen near large cities, many people may be killed and many buildings knocked down. Fires may start and do more damage than the quake itself.

Earthquakes come from a shaking of the rocks under the surface of the earth. Forces within the earth push against the rocks until they break. Sometimes, the earth above the break will split open.

We cannot always tell when an earthquake is coming. But we do know the places on the earth where they happen most often. Much damage is stopped by building stronger buildings in these places.

Many, many earthquakes may happen in a year. But most of them do no damage, for they happen under the sea.

E-8 Testing Yourself **NUMBER RIGHT**

1. Most earthquakes happen under the _____.

   Draw a line under the right answer.

2. From the story you can tell that
   a. earthquakes happen often.   b. all earthquakes cause damage.
      c. fires always happen along with earthquakes.

3. The story as a whole is about
   a. earthquakes under the sea.   c. people killed by earthquakes.
   b. earthquakes.   d. damage in cities.

4. Some earthquakes start fires in cities.   Yes   No   Does not say

5. All earthquakes do much harm.   Yes   No   Does not say

6. What word in line five of the story means **harm?** _____

How People Got Medicine

In old times, people and animals lived as friends. They worked together and helped each other.

But then the number of people grew. They wanted more of the world for themselves. The animals went farther back into the forest. They went into the places where people did not want to live. Hunters began to kill animals for meat. They wanted their skins for clothes.

The animals began to worry. "We must do something," they said. "We must learn how to protect ourselves."

One by one, each group of animals got together. First the bears called a meeting. They planned to make war on the hunters. But, they wondered, how could bears fight hunters with only their claws?

"We must have bows and arrows," one bear said. So the bears made bows and arrows. Then they tried to shoot the arrows from the bows, but they found that their claws got in the way. Some of the bears tried cutting off their claws. Now they could shoot better.

Soon the other bears started to cut off their claws, too. But Old White Bear asked, "If you cut off your claws, how can you climb trees?" The bears were sad, but they gave up their bows and arrows.

The deer had a meeting next. They planned that anyone who killed a deer would get a sickness unless the person asked pardon for the act. The deer sent word to the nearest camp of hunters to tell them

of the plan. These hunters sent the message to other hunters. Ever since that time, a hunter who kills a deer must ask for pardon.

Next came meetings of the fish and the reptiles. They planned to strike the hunters with bad dreams.

The birds and the insects also met. They planned to strike the hunters with different sicknesses.

But all this time, the trees and plants in the forest were listening to the plans of the animals. They did not like what they heard. People had not hurt the plants. Instead, the people had helped them. People dug the ground and watered it so that plants could grow better.

So the plants made a plan of their own to help the people. For every sickness given by the animals, the plants would bring a cure. Each kind of plant, from large trees to very small moss, was given a part to play.

In this way, the plants became the medicine which helped to end the sicknesses of people.

MY READING TIME _____ (400 WORDS)

Thinking It Over

1. Did the hunters have a right to kill animals for food?

2. If the bears had been able to shoot arrows at the hunters, would that have been a good plan?

3. Do you think the people were being good to the plants when they dug the ground and watered it?

Adapted from Amy Cruse, *The Young Folk's Book of Myths*. Boston: Little, Brown, and Co., 1927; pages 141–145.

Getting Ready for the Next Story

SAY AND KNOW

mechanics
machines
factories
equipment
army
soldiers
engineers
careers

Draw a line under each right answer.

1. People who serve in the army are called
   mechanics   engineers   soldiers.

2. It means **a place where cars are fixed or parked.**
   garage   machine   house

3. **People who work on cars and machines** are
   cowpokes   mechanics   cooks.

4. Factories are places where people   **sleep   eat   make things.**

5. If you **work at a job**, you have a   **machine   factory   career**.

F-1   New Jobs for Women

Many years ago, only men were mechanics. Women could not get jobs working with machines.

During World War II, people's ideas about women's work began to change. When men were sent to war, women took their places in factories and shops. They helped build the ships that took food

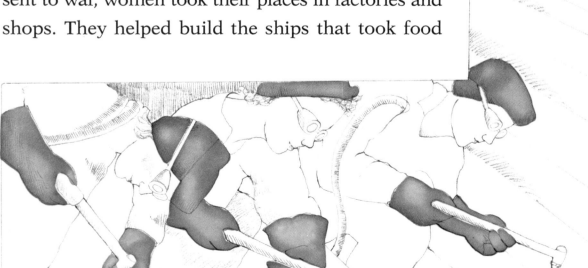

and equipment to the army across the seas. They worked in factories to make guns for the soldiers.

After the war, women continued to work at all sorts of jobs. Today, women are police officers, engineers, and mechanics. They build houses, they repair cars, and they work in offices.

So girls today can look forward to a choice of many kinds of careers!

F-1   Testing Yourself   **NUMBER RIGHT**

1. During World War II, women worked in _____.

Draw a line under the right answer.

2. From the story you can tell that
   a. women have a wider choice of jobs now than they once did.
   b. women can get fewer jobs now than they used to.
   c. only boys can work with machines.

3. The story as a whole is about
   a. jobs for men.   c. working in factories.
   b. jobs for women.   d. building houses.

4. Before World War II, women did not work as mechanics.

Yes   No   Does not say

5. Only women worked in factories and shops during World War II.

Yes   No   Does not say

6. What word in the second sentence of the story means **kinds of work**?

_____

Getting Ready for the Next Story

SAY AND KNOW

lumberjacks
loggers
forests
axes
crosscut
machines
hearty
eaters
easily
tales

Draw a line under the right word or fill in the blanks.

1. Someone who cuts logs is   a forest   a logger   an ax.

2. It means **not hard.**   machine   hearty   easily

3. It means **strong and well.**   hearty   machine   eaters

4. It means **stories.**   lumberjacks   crosscut   tales

5. Write the word that **eater** comes from. _____

6. Write the three-letter word in **logger.** _____

F-2   Lumberjack or Logger

When our country was young, all who worked in the forests cutting down trees did their work by hand. These people, or lumberjacks, had to use axes or crosscut saws. They wore bright colors in the woods so they could be easily seen.

94

It took big, strong people to do this work; so they were hearty eaters. They liked to sing and tell tall tales when their long day's work was done.

Today, most of the people who work in the forests use machines to cut down the trees. These lumberjacks are sometimes called loggers.

Whether we call them lumberjacks or loggers, they still are hearty eaters. They still like to tell tall tales. And they still wear bright clothes in the woods so that they can be seen from far away.

F-2   Testing Yourself   **NUMBER RIGHT**

1. People who used to work in the forests used crosscut saws or _____.

Draw a line under the right answer.

2. From the story you can tell that
    a. lumberjacks are different from loggers.
    b. trees must be cut down by hand.
    c. if lumberjacks could not be easily seen, they might be in danger.

3. The story as a whole is about
    a. axes and saws.   c. those who work in our forests.
    b. big eaters.   d. what lumberjacks wear.

4. Lumberjacks are people who cut down trees.   Yes   No   Does not say

5. Loggers still do most of their work by hand.   Yes   No   Does not say

6. What word in line four of the story means **tools for chopping?**

_____

Getting Ready for the Next Story

crane

tear

rip

crash

wreck

housewrecker

important

removed

Draw a line under the right word or fill in the blanks.

1. It means about the same as **tear.**   **rip**   crash   crane

2. It is **a sudden, loud sound.**   wreck   **crash**   wash

3. It is **a machine for moving things.**   tear   **crane**   smash

4. It means **having much meaning.**   rip   smash   **important**

5. Write another word for **taken away.** _____

6. Write the two words that make **housewrecker.**

_____   _____

F-3   Rip! Smash! Crash!

Some people work at putting up houses. Other people work at tearing houses down. These people are called housewreckers. They must take a building apart and move all the pieces away.

Sometimes, housewreckers use a big crane to help them in their work. The crane has a heavy ball swinging from its arm. The swinging ball rips, smashes, and crashes to make the building fall. The wreckers must be careful that no falling bricks, wood, or glass will hurt anyone. Heavy trucks are used to carry the pieces away.

96

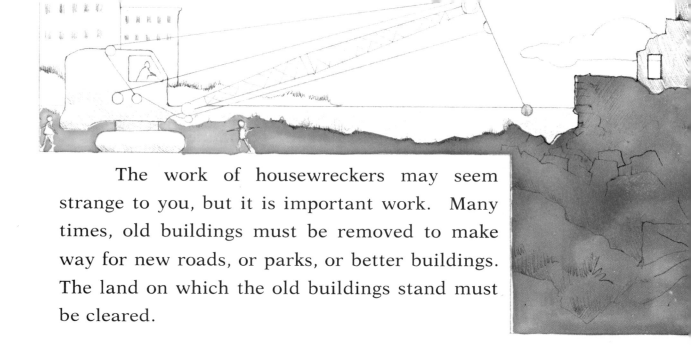

The work of housewreckers may seem strange to you, but it is important work. Many times, old buildings must be removed to make way for new roads, or parks, or better buildings. The land on which the old buildings stand must be cleared.

F-3 Testing Yourself   NUMBER RIGHT

1. **People who remove old buildings** are called _____.

   Draw a line under the right answer.

2. From the story you can tell that
     a. it is not easy to wreck a house.
     b. it is harder to wreck a house than to build it.
     c. it is easier to wreck a house than to build it.

3. The story as a whole is about
     a. how cranes work.   c. old buildings.
     b. new buildings.   d. an unusual kind of work.

4. People who build houses take them down, too.   Yes   No   Does not say

5. Housewreckers just smash things up and let them fall where they may.
                                   Yes   No   Does not say

6. What word in line fourteen of the story means **odd** or **unusual?**

   _____

Getting Ready for the Next Story

SAY AND KNOW

architects

designed

computer

blueprint

exactly

measurements

worth

Draw a line under each right answer or fill in the blank.

1. **People who design buildings** are called
   workers   computers   architects.

2. It means **in the same way.**   exactly   train   designed

3. A **blueprint** is **a**   computer   drawing   door.

4. It begins like **work.**   size   shape   worth

5. It means the same as **planned.**   played   designed   say

6. To find out **the size of things**, you take _____.

F-4   At the Drawing Board

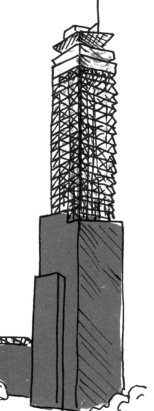

Look at the office buildings and houses around you. Do you know how they developed as they did? People called architects designed them. Architects think of how they want a building or house to look. Then they draw the plans to show every part of the building or house.

Architects draw their plans on paper and they also use computers. The plans are called a blueprint, which shows where the rooms, windows, doors, and stairs will be. The blueprint shows the size and shape of everything exactly as it will look.

The blueprint is like a map. People follow a map to get somewhere. Builders follow a blueprint to put a building or house together. So a blueprint must show the correct measurements.

Architects also design bridges. And sometimes architects change buildings that are already standing. So architects need to learn a lot of different things. It takes a lot of training. But if you talk to men and women who are architects, they will say it is worth it.

F-4 Testing Yourself   **NUMBER RIGHT**

1. An architect's plan is called a _____.

   Draw a line under the right answer.

2. From the story you can tell that
      a. architects don't enjoy their work.
      b. architects must be very careful when making a blueprint.
      c. architects need computers.

3. The story as a whole is about
      a. how to build a house.   c. an architect's job.
      b. using a map.   d. using a computer.

4. Architects go through a lot of training.   Yes   No   Does not say

5. Only women are architects.   Yes   No   Does not say

6. What word in sentence fourteen of the story means **right**? _____

Getting Ready for the Next Story

SAY AND KNOW   Draw a line under each right answer or fill in the blanks.

mountains

avalanche

loose

sheets

bury

snowslide

explosion

1. It makes a big noise and shakes or bursts things.

    sheets   explosion   loose

2. It means **snowslide.   snow   avalanche   bury**

3. It means **to become separate from.   fast   loose   will**

4. It means **cover over.   but   get   bury**

5. It begins like **sheep.   avalanche   sheets   snowslide**

6. Write the two words that join to make the word **snowslide.**

    _____   _____

F-5   An Exploding Job

There are many places on Earth that contain lots of snow. When there are mountains blanketed with snow, there is often a chance for an avalanche. An avalanche happens when pieces of rocks or snow get loose and slide down a mountainside.

The snow on a mountain glides down in big

white sheets. The sheets collect more snow and get bigger and bigger. They move faster and faster. Often the snow will bury houses, roads, and people.

Is there any way to stop an avalanche? No. But some people work at making an avalanche happen. Why? It is safer to make snow slide a little at a time than to have a big snowslide all at once.

The way these people make an avalanche is to set off an explosion. The explosion makes the snow come loose and begin to slide. Because the explosion was planned, the snowslide is safer. What a way to work!

F-5 Testing Yourself   **NUMBER RIGHT**

1. Sliding rock or snow is called an _____.

   Draw a line under the right answer.

2. From the story you can tell that
   a. there is not much snow on mountains.
   b. people like avalanches.
   c. making avalanches happen is a dangerous job.

3. The story as a whole is about
   a. avalanches.   c. how cold it is on a mountain.
   b. how to set an explosion.   d. how to bury a house in snow.

4. Avalanches happen in the mountains.   Yes   No   Does not say

5. Explosions always stop big avalanches.   Yes   No   Does not say

6. What word in the second sentence means **very high hills**?

Getting Ready for the Next Story

SAY AND KNOW

disease

regular

college

medicine

veterinarian

heart

doctor

operate

diet

hospital

Draw a line under the right word or fill in the blanks.

1. Someone who is **a doctor for animals** is

a veterinarian   an officer   a teacher.

2. It **pumps blood through the body.**   lungs   arms   heart

3. Doctors sometimes give medicine to people to make them

sick   well   tired.

4. A doctor usually operates in a   school   hospital   tent.

5. Another word for **sickness** is _____.

6. The school you go to after high school is _____.

F-6   Animal Doctors

Do you have a pet? Do you like to take care
of animals?

Girls and boys who like animals may want
to study to be veterinarians. Veterinarians, often

102

called "vets," are animal doctors. Many work in animal hospitals. Others may work on farms or at a zoo. Some study animal diseases and try to find ways to keep the animals from getting sick. They search for medicine to cure sick animals.

Vets are like regular doctors. They listen to an animal's heart. They check its ears, eyes, mouth, and blood. They operate when they need to. They may give the animal shots and tell the pet's owner what diet is best.

Girls and boys who want to be vets should plan to go to college for two years and then to vet school for four years more.

F-6 Testing Yourself   **NUMBER RIGHT**

1. Veterinarians are doctors who treat _____.

   Draw a line under the right answer.

2. From the story you can tell that
   a. not all vets treat pets.   b. vets do not treat wild animals.
                    c. vets do not have to go to college.

3. The story as a whole is about
   a. medicine for sick animals.   b. how to care for pets.
                    c. what vets do.

4. Vets need six years of school after high school.   Yes   No   Does not say

5. Vets are different from veterinarians.   Yes   No   Does not say

6. What word in line four of the story means **to learn?** _____

Getting Ready for the Next Story

burned

ladder

connect

action

fighters

overcome

hose

breathing

Draw a line under the right word or fill in the blanks.

1. It means **to put together.**   hold   connect   action

2. It is **something that carries water.**   job   hose   ladder

3. It means **hurt by fire.**   action   breathing   burned

4. It is **a thing to climb on.**   ladder   hose   action

5. Write **breathe** with an **ing** ending. _____

6. Write the first four-letter word in **overcome.** _____

F-7   They Have to Be Fast!

Fire fighters have to work fast. When the fire bell rings, they have to jump up, get on their truck, and get to the fire as fast as they can. As soon as the truck stops, the fire fighters spring into action.

Some connect the hose. Others put up the ladders. Others get ready to run up the ladders with hoses and axes. Each one has a job to do, and each job has to be done fast.

Besides putting out the fire, these men and women have to give help to people who are burned or hurt. They must know how to help people who are overcome by smoke. They do this by giving the people help in breathing.

Fast work by fire fighters has saved many lives and many thousands of dollars.

F-7   Testing Yourself   NUMBER RIGHT

1. A fire fighter has to work _____.

    Draw a line under the right answer.

2. From the story you can tell that
    a. all fire fighters do many jobs at a fire.
    b. the faster fire fighters work, the less damage there is likely to be.
    c. a fire fighter does not need any special training.

3. This story as a whole is about
    a. what a fire fighter has to know.   c. fire trucks.
    b. fire fighters and their work.   d. how fast a fire fighter works.

4. Part of a fire fighter's job is to help people who are hurt.
                                    Yes   No   Does not say

5. Fire fighters must know how to help people who are overcome by smoke.
                                    Yes   No   Does not say

6. What word in line four of the story means **to leap** or **jump?**

Getting Ready for the Next Story

SAY AND KNOW

lookout
ranger
soil
protected
insects
disease
destroyed

Draw a line under each right answer or fill in the blank.

1. It means **kept safe.**   destroyed   protected   worked

2. It means **a forest guard.**   insects   radio   ranger

3. It is the same as **sickness.**   smoke   disease   snail

4. It means **ruined.**   looked   destroyed   planted

5. Write the two words in **lookout.** _____ _____

6. Write the word that means **bugs.** _____

F-8   On the Lookout

A forest ranger's life is a busy one. Part of the job is caring for the trees in the forest where the ranger works. The soil below the trees and the animals around them are all in the care of the forest ranger. Each year, some trees must be cut. New trees must be planted. Trees must be protected from insects, disease, and fire.

Many of our beautiful forests would be destroyed by fires if it were not for the quick work of the forest rangers. In dry weather, one ranger

must be on the lookout for fire all the time.

Forest rangers also have another job. They must protect the animals. And they must teach people how to visit without bothering the animals that live in the forest.

F-8   Testing Yourself   **NUMBER RIGHT**

1. Part of the ranger's work is to watch for _____.

Draw a line under the right answer.

2. From the story you can tell that
    a. the work of the ranger goes on all the time.
    b. it is the job of the lookout to fight a forest fire.
    c. one ranger can usually put out a fire.

3. The story as a whole is about
    a. fighting forest fires.   c. the work that rangers do.
    b. cutting and planting trees.   d. our beautiful forests.

4. Part of a ranger's work is to make sure no trees are cut.
                                Yes   No   Does not say

5. The only thing that rangers do is to watch for fires.   Yes   No   Does not say

6. What word in the first sentence of the story means **full of things to do**?

_____

How the Animals Stole Springtime

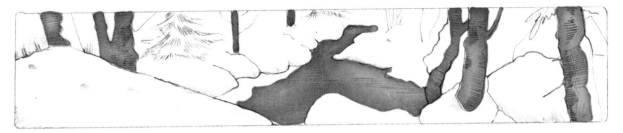

There was a time when the seasons were kept at a village, tied up in deerskin bags. The Chief could let them out for as long as he wanted.

The Chief liked Winter best of all. Sometimes, Winter would stay out for two years at a time!

One year, the Chief let Winter out and would not call it back. Winter stayed and stayed. The snow grew very deep. The animals could not find food, no matter how hard they tried.

"If Spring does not come soon, we will not be able to find food," said the bear.

The wolf said, "We will have to steal Spring and let it out of the bag."

"But how?" asked the squirrel. "It hangs inside the lodge of the Chief. Who can walk too softly to be heard? Who can run too quickly to be caught?"

"What no one of us can do alone, all may do together," said the wolf.

Then the wolf pointed to Softest-Walker, Farthest-Thrower, and Strongest-One. "The three of you together can do this thing. Come. I will tell you how."

So they started out across the deep, white snow. By the time they came to the village, each knew what to do.

Strongest-One and the wolf waited up on the hill. The other two went on.

Near the lodge of the Chief, Farthest-Thrower stopped. Now only Softest-Walker went alone.

Softly, softly, she went into the lodge. Summer, Autumn, and Spring were hanging there in bags.

Softly, she took Spring down and carried it from the lodge.

As she came out, the Old One, who watched the lodge, saw her. "Hi-ee! Hi-ee!" the Old One called. "They are stealing Spring!"

The people came running from the lodge. Now Softest-Walker did not walk any more. She ran to Farthest-Thrower and handed the bag to him.

Farthest-Thrower knew what he must do. He threw the bag with a great throw to the two on the hill.

Strongest-One caught the bag with Spring inside. She pulled at it with all her might. *R-r-rip!* it opened.

Warm winds rushed out. Spring filled the air. When the others got up the hill, the snow was melting.

That is how the animals stole Spring. And, who knows? If they had not, it might be Winter still.

MY READING TIME _____ (400 WORDS)

Thinking It Over

1. There is an old saying, "In unity (oneness) there is strength." What did the wolf say that means the same thing?

2. Could Softest-Walker or Farthest-Thrower or Strongest-One have stolen Spring alone? Tell why you say yes or no.

Adapted with permission of Charles Scribner's Sons from *Kootenai Why Stories* by Frank B. Linderman, copyright, 1926, Charles Scribner's Sons; renewal copyright, 1954, Wilder J. Linderman, Verne B. Linderman, and Norma L. Waller.

Getting Ready for the Next Story

SAY AND KNOW

Draw a line under the right word or fill in the blank.

earth

trade

paces

ruler

measure

clock

scales

distance

1. They tell how heavy something is. **scales**   **trades**   **clocks**

2. It tells how long something is. **clock**   **earth**   **ruler**

3. It tells what time it is. **scales**   **ruler**   **clock**

4. **To tell how much is to**   **trade**   **measure**   **pace.**

5. **From here to there is a**   **ruler**   **trade**   **distance.**

6. Three **steps** would be three _____.

G-1   From Here to There

Almost as soon as there were people on Earth, they found they needed to measure things. They needed to know how long things were. But there were no rulers. They needed to tell time. But there were no clocks.

They wanted to know how much of something they had when they wanted to trade. But there were no scales to use. They needed to know how long and how wide the land they farmed was. But they had no good way to tell.

At first, people could measure distance only by steps. They might say that they lived ten paces from the river. Or, to tell time, they might say that a trip would start at sunup.

110

But, little by little, people found better ways to measure. They thought of ways to find out what they needed to know.

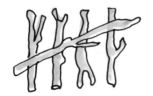

G-1   Testing Yourself   **NUMBER RIGHT**

1. Early people soon needed to _____ things.

Draw a line under the right answer.

2. From the story you can tell that
  a. paces are the same as steps.
  b. to tell time, early people used clocks.
  c. early people knew how long a yard was.

3. The story as a whole is about
  a. measuring how long things were.   c. early ways of measuring.
  b. measuring distances by steps.   d. clocks and scales.

4. Early people had a way of telling time by the sun.

                                    Yes   No   Does not say

5. Rulers are one foot in length.   Yes   No   Does not say

6. What word in line two of the story means **our world?** _____.

Getting Ready for the Next Story

inch

pace

stretch.

measure

width

thumb

Draw a line under the right word or fill in the blank.

1. It is **how wide a thing is.**   weight   **width**   length

2. It is shorter than a foot.   mile   **inch**   yard

3. It is part of your hand.   leg   pace   **thumb**

4. To stretch is to   **reach out**   pull in   breathe.

5. Write the letter you do not hear in **pace.** _____

G-2   Legs, Hands, and Thumbs

At first, people used their legs to tell how far away something was. From one place to another was so many steps, or paces.

Sometimes, they wanted to measure something very short. Then they used the width of their thumb. The thumb measure was about one inch.

112

For something a little longer, they used the width of their hands. Each hand was about four inches. Hands were used to tell how tall horses were.

Sometimes, the thing was longer than a hand but shorter than a pace. Then people used a foot. A foot came to be twelve inches.

Another measure was the yard. Stretch out your arm. From your nose to the end of your thumb is about one yard. It is about the same as a pace.

G-2 Testing Yourself

NUMBER RIGHT

1. What was used to tell the height of horses? _____

Draw a line under the right answer.

2. From the story you can tell that
    a. the little finger was used in measuring.
    b. a hand is about four thumbs wide.
    c. a pace was a foot long.

3. The story as a whole is about
    a. yards and feet.   c. using parts of the body to measure things.
    b. thumbs and fingers.   d. using steps to measure distance.

4. We still measure the height of horses by hands today.
                                      Yes   No   Does not say

5. A foot is longer than a hand.   Yes   No   Does not say

6. What word in line five comes from the word **wide**? _____

Getting Ready for the Next Story

SAY AND KNOW

decide

bodies

royal

problem

person

length

size

Draw a line under the right word or fill in the blanks.

1. It is **how long a thing is.**   length   width   weight

2. You try to solve a   **length**   **problem**   **person.**

3. When you make up your mind, you   **measure**   **decide**   **talk.**

4. Arms, legs, and heads are parts of   **bodies**   **weight**   **feet.**

5. A man or a woman is a _____.

6. The foot of a king or queen is the _____ foot.

G-3   The Royal Foot

Early people measured things by using parts of their bodies. They used fingers and hands. They used arms and feet.

But this plan did not work well enough. Some people were large. Others were small. Some had big hands and feet. Others did not. A

114

few had very long legs and took longer steps than others. So inches and feet and yards and paces were not always the same.

So people decided to use just one person. The King or Queen was often picked. A foot was the length of the royal foot. An inch was the width of the royal thumb.

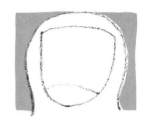

But when a ruler died, the problem came back. The new ruler was not the same size as the old one. So the measures had to be changed once again.

G-3 Testing Yourself   NUMBER RIGHT

1. Whose foot was often used as a measure? _____

Draw a line under the right answer.

2. From the story you can tell that
    a. using the royal foot solved all the problems.
    b. feet and arms do not make very good measures.
    c. kings and queens are all about the same size.

3. The story as a whole is about
    a. making fixed measures.   c. fingers and feet.
    b. long legs and feet.   d. inches and feet.

4. Some countries still have kings and queens today.
                                      Yes   No   Does not say

5. Some rulers were large and some were small.   Yes   No   Does not say

6. What word in line eleven means **chosen?** _____

Getting Ready for the Next Story

SAY AND KNOW

double

measures

paces

trouble

different

understanding

Draw a line under the right word or fill in the blanks.

1. It means **not the same.**　alike　trouble　**different**

2. It means **a hard time.**　measures　double　**trouble**

3. It means **twice as much.**　single　**double**　many

4. Write the word that begins **understanding.** _____

5. It rhymes with **faces.** _____

G-4　How Long Is a Mile?

People in one part of the world used one set of measures.　But people in other places used other measures.

In Rome, a mile was one thousand double paces.　In England, it was five thousand two hundred eighty feet if you were on land.　But it was six thousand eighty feet if you were on water.

In Germany, there was a "long mile."　There was also a "short mile."　In one country, the mile was only three thousand six hundred feet.　In another, it was ten times as long—

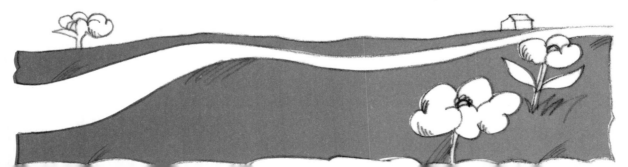

thirty-six thousand feet. A mile was not the same for people from different parts of the world.

Inches were different too. In one place, an inch was a thumb's width. In another, it was the length of the first joint of the thumb.

So people from different parts of the world had trouble understanding each other when they talked about miles and inches.

G-4   Testing Yourself

1. What was used to measure a mile in Rome? _____ _____

Draw a line under the right answer.

2. From the story you can tell that
   a. in England, a mile on land was shorter than a mile on water.
   b. in Germany, the miles were all "long miles."
   c. in Rome, a mile was one thousand feet.

3. The story as a whole is about
   a. different kinds of feet and yards.   c. miles in Rome.
   b. different kinds of inches and miles.   d. thumbs and inches.

4. A mile is still thirty-six thousand feet in one country.

                    Yes   No   Does not say

5. Countries no longer use miles to measure distances.

                    Yes   No   Does not say

6. What word in line thirteen means **not the same**? _____

Getting Ready for the Next Story

SAY AND KNOW

president

confused

worth

colony

shapes

system

measures

Draw a line under the right word or fill in the blank.

1. **A way of working is a**   system   worth   coin.

2. A baseball and a football have different

coins   shapes   systems.

3. **The head of our country is the**

president   king   principal.

4. If you are mixed up, you are   worth   measures   confused.

5. If you know the prices of things, you know their

worth   shapes   sizes.

6. It has a sound like the **oll** in **doll**. _____

G-5   What Is It Worth?

As you know, at one time, different countries used different measures. But even inside the same country, measures were not always the same.

When America was very young, each colony had its own money. The coins that were used in different places were not the same sizes. They were not the same shapes. They did not have the same worth.

Money from other countries was also used. Some was from England. Other money came from Spain, France, and Portugal.

118

People became confused. They would buy things. But they could not be sure if they had their money's worth.

Then one of our first presidents, Thomas Jefferson, thought of a good plan. He started the dollar system. It was based on counting by tens. Ten cents made a dime. Ten dimes made a dollar. Today we still use Jefferson's plan.

G-5   Testing Yourself   **NUMBER RIGHT**

1. There were so many different kinds of money that people became

_____ .

Draw a line under the right answer.

2. From the story you can tell that
    a. the money from England was worth more than the money from Spain.
    b. the coins were all the same sizes.
    c. people might pay more for things than they were worth.

3. The story as a whole is about
    a. American colonies.   c. Thomas Jefferson.
    b. English money.   d. our money system.

4. Thomas Jefferson was the second American president.
                             Yes   No   Does not say

5. Americans once used money from France.   Yes   No   Does not say

6. What word in line ten of the story means **lands?** _____

Getting Ready for the Next Story

discovery

million

metric

meter

scientist

divided

system

equator

Draw a line under the right word or fill in the blank.

1. A person who studies science is a
metric   system   scientist.

2. When something has been cut into pieces, it has been
eaten   added   divided.

3. When you find something new, it is a
system   discovery   meter.

4. It is a very large number.   **million**   ten   metric

5. Write the word that comes from the word **meter.** _____

G-6   A New System

Almost two hundred years ago, scientists in France were not happy. They thought they had to have a better way of measuring things. When they used the old ways, they found it hard to talk with people in other countries about their discoveries.

So these scientists started a new system. It was based on what they called a meter. They said the meter would be a part of the distance from the North Pole to the equator. They divided this long distance by ten million. They called one of these parts a meter.

120

The meter turned out to be a little longer than a yard. A yard is thirty-six inches. A meter is a little over thirty-nine inches.

This was the beginning of the metric system. It is now used in almost all countries.

G-6 Testing Yourself   **NUMBER RIGHT**

1. A meter is _____ than a yard.

Draw a line under the right answer.

2. From the story you can tell that
   a. scientists never understand each other.   b. a meter is ten feet.
        c. using meters instead of yards helps scientists.

3. The story as a whole is about
   a. the start of the metric system.   c. scientists.
   b. the distance to the North Pole.   d. ten million meters.

4. The meter is exactly thirty-nine inches.   Yes   No   Does not say

5. All countries now use only the metric system.   Yes   No   Does not say

6. What word in line ten means **the imaginary line around the middle of the**

   earth? _____

Getting Ready for the Next Story

kilometers

half

hundred

centimeters

thousand

inch

distance

decimeters

Draw a line under the right word or fill in the blanks.

1. A thousand meters are a   **kilometer**   **mile**   **yard.**

2. Each part of a pie that has been cut into two equal parts is a
         quarter   **third**   **half.**

3. Ten hundreds are a   **thousand**   **million**   **century.**

4. A small part of a meter is   **an inch**   **a foot**   **a centimeter.**

5. Write the three words that have **meters** in them.

_____ _____ _____

G-7   Tens, Hundreds, Thousands

We build the metric system on tens. It is like our money system. A dollar is one hundred cents. A meter, in the same way, is one hundred centimeters. A kilometer is one thousand meters.

Centimeters are like inches. They measure small things. It takes about two and a half centimeters to make an inch.

Kilometers are like miles. They are used to measure long distances. A kilometer is a little more than half a mile.

It is easy to use metric measures because they are in tens, hundreds, or thousands. When you use inches, you have to know many different units. You have to know that twelve inches are a foot. Three feet, or thirty-six inches, make a yard. A mile is five thousand two hundred eighty feet or one thousand seven hundred eighty yards.

But with meters, ten centimeters make a decimeter. Ten decimeters make a meter. A thousand meters make a kilometer.

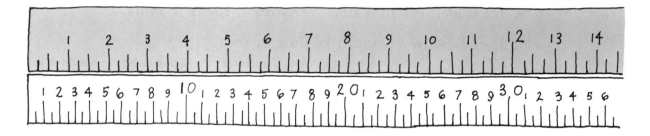

1. Ten decimeters make a _____.

2. From the story you can tell that
    a. centimeters are longer than feet.
    b. inches and feet are no longer used.
    c. kilometers per hour tell how fast you are going.

3. The story as a whole is about
    a. dollars and meters.   c. measuring distances.
    b. the system of tens.   d. centimeters and inches.

4. A yard is thirty-six inches.   Yes   No   Does not say

5. An inch is longer than a centimeter.   Yes   No   Does not say

6. What word in line one of the story means **to make** or **put together**?

_____

Getting Ready for the Next Story

SAY AND KNOW   Draw a line under the right word or words.

freezing

invent

absolute

thermometer

degrees

century

zero

melt

1. **A century** is   **one hundred years**   **a story**   **ten years.**

2. On a thermometer, **zero** is **a**
   low point   **middle point**   **high point.**

3. When you make something new, you   **invent**   **melt**   **freeze.**

4. **Degrees** are marks on a   **ruler**   **meter**   **thermometer.**

5. Ice that turns to water   **freezes**   **melts**   **boils.**

6. It ends with a sound like **flute** or **toot**
   century   **absolute**   **measure.**

G-8   Hot and Cold

We have seen that people learned to tell how long things were. They also needed to know how hot or cold things were. The tool that measures heat is a thermometer.

More than two hundred fifty years ago, a German scientist named Fahrenheit invented a thermometer. He said the freezing point of salt water would be zero degrees. On this thermometer, fresh water freezes at thirty-two degrees. It boils at two hundred twelve degrees.

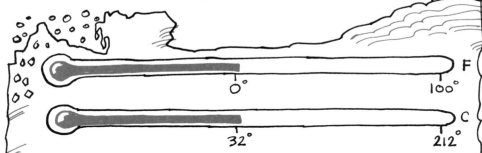

124

Most countries using the metric system do not use the Fahrenheit thermometer. They use the Celsius thermometer. It was made in 1742 by Celsius, a Swedish scientist. On this thermometer, ice melts at zero degrees. Water boils at one hundred degrees.

Another thermometer is the Kelvin. It was made by a British scientist in the last century. Only scientists use it. It starts at absolute zero. This is a point where there is no heat at all.

G-8   Testing Yourself

NUMBER RIGHT

1. The _____ tells how hot or cold things are.

Draw a line under the right answer.

2. From the story you can tell that
    a. there is more than one way to measure heat.
    b. salt water freezes at thirty-two degrees on the Fahrenheit thermometer.
    c. the Celsius thermometer was invented about one hundred years ago.

3. The story as a whole is about
    a. the Fahrenheit thermometer.   c. different kinds of thermometers.
    b. the Celsius and Kelvin   d. scientists.
       thermometers.

4. The Kelvin thermometer can measure very great heat and very great cold.
                              Yes   No   Does not say

5. The Fahrenheit, Celsius, and Kelvin thermometers were all invented by scientists.   Yes   No   Does not say

6. What word in line fifteen means **frozen water?** _____

Why the Sun Comes Up Slowly

In the early days, long gone by, it once grew very hot. Week after week, the sun came down, hotter and hotter. Green things turned dry and brown. Animals fell by the way, for they could find no food.

"It is not right for the sun to do this," the rabbit said. "I am brave. I am not afraid of the sun. I will take my bow and my arrows and shoot it."

So the foolish rabbit took a bow and some arrows and set out on the way. After many a day, the rabbit came to the place where the sun rose.

When the time came for the sun to show its face, the rabbit was ready. *Zing!* The arrow flew on its way.

But the sun knew the rabbit's plan. It moved out of the way. It came up farther to the south. The arrow missed the sun.

The sun laughed at the rabbit. Now it came down down hotter than ever.

"I will get the sun to-morrow," the rabbit said. "I

know the very spot where it came up."

Again, the next morning, the sun moved to the south. Again, the rabbit's arrow missed the sun. Day after day, the sun tricked the rabbit. Each day it moved to the side.

Then, at last, the rabbit learned the trick. The sun was coming up each day a little way south of where it had been on the

day before. The next day, the rabbit held the arrow just that much to the side. When the sun came up, *Zing!* The rabbit's arrow went into the face of the sun.

The rabbit laughed for joy. "I have killed the sun! Look! See how brave I am!"

Then the rabbit looked at the sun and was afraid. Fire was running out of the hole in the sun. All the world was on fire!

Then the rabbit said, "How foolish I have been! I must run as fast as I can to get away from the fire of the sun."

Even after the fire went out, the rabbit kept on running. From that time on, the rabbit has been a very frightened animal. And the sun comes up slowly and looks all around before it shows its full face. It wants to be sure no one is waiting to shoot it with an arrow.

MY READING TIME _____ **(400 WORDS)**

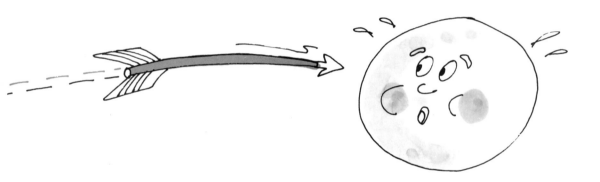

Thinking It Over

1. Was the rabbit brave or just foolish?

2. What did the rabbit do that was smart?

3. What would one learn from this old Native American story of how things came to be?

Adapted with permission of Prentice-Hall, Inc., Englewood Cliffs, N.J., from *Why the North Star Stands Still* by William R. Palmer. Copyright, 1946, 1957, by William R. Palmer.

Getting Ready for the Next Story

SAY AND KNOW

hobby
spend
collect
collecting
studying
helpful
interesting
course

Draw a line under the right word.

1. **Of course** means   **naturally   useful   fun.**

2. It rhymes with **lend.   helpful   spend   turn**

3. It means **gathering together.   interest   spend   collecting**

4. It means about the same as **learning.**
                                           trying   studying   making

5. It is **a special interest.   better   course   hobby**

H-1   Time Out for Fun

A hobby is something you like to spend time on just for fun. Some people have fun doing one thing. Other people have fun doing other things. Doing things can be a hobby. Collecting things can be a hobby. Making things can be a hobby. Studying things can be a hobby.

A hobby does not have to be important to anyone but you. It does not have to be useful or helpful. It does not have to bring you money. It just has to be very interesting to you.

Sometimes, of course, hobbies do turn out to be useful or helpful. Some, even, do make money. But that does not make them better hobbies than those which people have just for fun. Do you have a hobby?

H-1 Testing Yourself   **NUMBER RIGHT**

1. Something you do just for fun is called a _____.

   Draw a line under the right answer.

2. From the story you can tell that
   a. some hobbies are good and some are bad.
   b. people enjoy working on their hobbies.
   c. hobbies waste time.

3. The story as a whole is about
   a. collecting things.   c. studying things.
   b. making things.   d. what a hobby is.

4. Studying something is a poor hobby.   Yes   No   Does not say

5. The best hobbies are those that help you make money.
                                    Yes   No   Does not say

6. What word in line four of the story means **gathering?**

   _____

Getting Ready for the Next Story

SAY AND KNOW

collector

stamps

president

hobby

popular

trade

trading

Draw a line under the right word or fill in the blank.

1. It begins with the same sound as **kind.**   **trade**   **trick**   **collector**

2. It means **well liked.**   **popular**   **pretty**   **wonderful**

3. Which word means **the head of a country?**
                hobby   **teacher**   **president**

4. It is **a sticker used to pay for mailing.**
                stamp   **trade**   **color**

5. Write the word that **collector** comes from. _____

H-2   Around the World with a Hobby

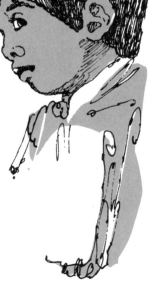

In every country of the world, there are people who like to collect stamps. Young people and old people, presidents and rulers collect stamps. It is one of the most popular hobbies in the world.

Stamp collecting started soon after the first stamp was made. Stamp collectors soon began

130

trading stamps with each other. They began to buy and sell the ones that were hard to find.

Many people collect only stamps with pictures of other places. Some collect stamps that come from only one country. Others collect stamps that show only birds or animals. You might collect only stamps that are all the same color.

No matter what kind of stamps you collect, stamp collecting can be fun.

H-2 Testing Yourself   **NUMBER RIGHT**

1. Someone who saves stamps is called a stamp _____.

   Draw a line under the right answer.

2. From the story you can tell that
   a. all stamp collections are alike.
   b. it is not always easy for a collector to find the wanted stamps.
   c. the best stamp collections have stamps of one color.

3. The story as a whole is about
   a. rulers and presidents.   c. trading stamps.
   b. the stamp collecting hobby.   d. stamps with pictures of birds.

4. Only children collect stamps.   Yes   No   Does not say

5. All collectors collect the same stamps.   Yes   No   Does not say

6. What word in line eight of the story means **exchanging things?**

   _____

Getting Ready for the Next Story

coin

dollar

exist

history

Abraham

Lincoln

money

Draw a line under the right word or fill in the blank.

1. History is the study of   **past times**   **old money**   **stamps.**

2. It is **one hundred cents.**   **penny**   **dollar**   **worth**

3. It has a sound like the **oy** in **boy.**   **dollar**   **box**   **coin**

4. It means **to be.**   **exist**   **collect**   **buy**

5. It has a starting sound like **hobby.**   **exist**   **honor**   **history**

6. Write the words that name a **president.** _____

_____

H-3   Pennies Worth Dollars

The first pennies made in our country were much bigger than our pennies today. Coin collectors say these first pennies are now worth many dollars.

Many coin collectors have Indian-head pennies in their collections. These coins were made for many years. Today, our pennies have a picture of Abraham Lincoln on one side.

Some people collect not only different kinds of pennies, but also pennies from different years. They may collect pennies the way other people collect stamps.

132

Coin collecting is a popular hobby all over the world. Many coins were once made by countries which do not exist today. Coins from such countries are hard to find.

Coin collecting can lead you to learn about the history of many countries.

H-3   Testing Yourself   NUMBER RIGHT

1. Today our pennies have a picture of _____.

Draw a line under the right answer.

2. From the story you can tell that
    a. coin collectors do not want old coins.
    b. coin collecting never costs the collector much.
    c. different countries have different coins.

3. The story as a whole is about
    a. popular hobbies.   c. the hobby of collecting coins.
    b. collecting pennies.   d. Indian-head pennies.

4. Old coins are not worth collecting, but new ones are.
                            Yes   No   Does not say

5. Coin collectors can learn a lot about history.   Yes   No   Does not say

6. What word in line thirteen of the story means **well liked?** _____

Getting Ready for the Next Story

SAY AND KNOW

puppet	
act	
cloth	
clay	
wax	
peanuts	
string	
strung	
person	
grown-up	

Draw a line under the right word or fill in the blank.

1. **A doll that is moved by a hand or by strings** is called **a**
   hobby   puppet   peanut.

2. It means **to play a part.**   jump   sing   act

3. Clothes are most often made of   **wax**   **string**   **cloth.**

4. It begins like **string.**   **pulling**   **clay**   **strung**

5. It is **a man, woman, or child.**   knee   act   person

6. Write the letter you do not hear in **grown-up.** _____

H-4   Not Just for Children

Puppet shows are not just for children. Even grown-ups like to make puppets and see puppet shows. Since long ago, puppet shows have been popular all over the world.

Puppets have been made of cloth, wood, paper, clay, wax, and stone. Some have even

been made of peanuts strung together and dressed in cloth.

Puppets can dance and walk and act the way people want them to. Some puppets are moved by a hand inside the puppet itself. Others are moved by a person pulling on wires or strings. The person who makes the puppet move also talks for it.

Making puppets is a hobby by itself. Putting on puppet shows is a hobby, too. If you like to act or put on shows, try puppets for a hobby.

H-4   Testing Yourself   NUMBER RIGHT

1. Some puppets are worked by hand, and some by _____.

   Draw a line under the right answer.

2. From the story you can tell that
   a. one person must talk for a puppet while another moves it.
   b. you can act out plays with puppets.
   c. you have to buy puppets if you want to put on puppet shows.

3. The story as a whole is about
   a. puppets as a hobby.   c. how to put on puppet shows.
   b. how to work puppets.   d. what puppets are made of.

4. Puppets move and talk by themselves.   Yes   No   Does not say

5. All puppets are made of wood.   Yes   No   Does not say

6. What word in line eleven of the story means **different ones?** _____

Getting Ready for the Next Story

model

copy

cardboard

architect

engineer

dam

bridge

transportation

Draw a line under the right word or fill in the blank.

1. **Something that is made to be just like another thing** is called **a** hobby copy transportation.

2. **A small copy** is called **a** hobby child model.

3. **It is a kind of heavy paper.** cardboard clay wood

4. **It has a sound like the k in kitchen.**

   architect chair know

5. **People who plan bridges** are engineers models dams.

6. Write the little word at the end of **cardboard.** _____

H-5 Just Like the Big Ones

Many people like to collect models of boats, airplanes, cars, or trains. A model is a small copy of something. Models of almost anything used for transportation are fun to collect.

Collecting models is a hobby for both young and old. Making the models is a good hobby, too. To some people, making models is more than a hobby. It is part of their work. Architects make models of large buildings. Each model shows how the real building will look when it is finished. Engineers make models of dams and bridges. Sometimes, models of parts of cities are made so

136

that streets and roads can be planned before the work is started.

Making models is a hobby that is fun for anyone. Even very young children can make models from paper, cardboard, wood, or clay.

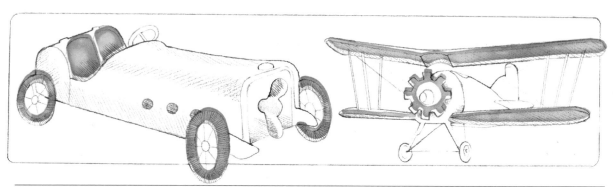

H-5   Testing Yourself

1. A model is a small _____.

Draw a line under the right answer.

2. From the story you can tell that
   a. making models is too hard for young people.
   b. models are made only as a hobby.
   c. models are very useful to people who build things.

3. The story as a whole is about
   a. money for model making.   c. model airplanes.
   b. collecting and making models.   d. people who use models.

4. Only architects or engineers make models.   Yes   No   Does not say

5. All models are made only of wood.   Yes   No   Does not say

6. What word in line eight of the story means **persons who plan buildings?**

_____

137

Getting Ready for the Next Story

SAY AND KNOW

Draw a line under the right word or fill in the blank.

bone

ivory

china

rubber

rag

corncobs

plastic

collection

1. It is **a soft stuff that will bounce.**   ivory   china   **rubber**

2. It is **fine, baked clay.**   ivory   rag   **china**

3. It ends like **stick.**   **corncobs**   plastic   collect

4. It begins like **ice.**   **ivory**   it   interest

5. They are **torn cloth.**   plastic   history   **rags**

6. Write the word from which **collection** comes. _____

H-6   All Kinds of Dolls

Does it surprise you that a boy or man as well as a girl or woman might like to collect dolls?

Dolls from different times and different places tell us much about the history and clothing of the world.   History interests both men and women.   That is why all kinds of people collect dolls.

138

Dolls have been made of bone or wood or ivory. Dolls have been made of rags, bark, corncobs, and sea shells. Years ago, dolls had china heads and bodies made of cloth. Later, many dolls were made of rubber. Today, most dolls in this country are made of plastic.

Some doll collectors look for dolls that come from different countries. Some save only one kind of doll, such as rag dolls. Do you know anyone who has a doll collection?

H-6   Testing Yourself   NUMBER RIGHT

1. Dolls can tell a lot about the _____ of the world.

Draw a line under the right answer.

2. From the story you can tell that
    a. history should be taught by using dolls.
    b. dolls may be made of almost any material.
    c. doll collectors collect only small dolls.

3. The story as a whole is about
    a. the history of dolls.   c. the fun of doll collecting.
    b. the history of the world.   d. what dolls are made of.

4. Only girls and women collect dolls.   Yes   No   Does not say

5. Long ago, dolls were made of plastic.   Yes   No   Does not say

6. What word in line eleven of the story means **fine, white, baked clay?**

_____

Getting Ready for the Next Story

carve

carving

knife

sculpture

outline

material

finger

Draw a line under the right word or fill in the blanks.

1. It means **to cut.**   finger   carve   draw

2. It begins like **school.**   sold   cold   sculpture

3. It begins with the sound of **one.**   only   wonderful   own

4. It is **a line to show the shape of something.** _____

5. Write the two letters you do not hear in **knife.** _____ _____

6. Write the word that means **what a thing is made from.**

_____

H-7   Another Use for Soap

A knife and a bar of soap are all you need for soap carving. First, make a drawing of the thing you want to carve. Copy your drawing on a piece of soap. Use a soft, white bar.

When the outline is drawn, use a small knife to cut away the soap around your drawing. If you make a sitting cat, your soap carving will show both sides of the cat. It will show the front and the back of it, too.

Carving out or modeling any material is called sculpture. When your soap sculpture is done, let it dry for a few days. Then rub it care-

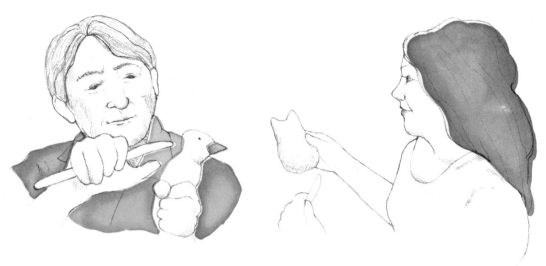

fully with a soft piece of paper.   Rub it with your
finger, too.   Rubbing will make your soap sculpture shine.   This hobby is wonderful fun.

H-7   Testing Yourself   **NUMBER RIGHT**

1. The carving out of any material is called _____.

Draw a line under the right answer.

2. From the story you can tell that
    a. soap sculptures cannot be made of colored soap.
    b. it takes a long time to make a soap sculpture.
    c. a soap sculpture is a small statue of something.

3. The story as a whole is about
    a. how to carve soap.   c. how to carve.
    b. how to draw a cat.   d. how to keep clean.

4. You need many things for a soap carving.   Yes   No   Does not say

5. Sculpture shows only one side of a thing.   Yes   No   Does not say

6. What word in line four of the story means **not hard?** _____

Getting Ready for the Next Story

SAY AND KNOW

pebble

form

forming

library

magnify

magnifying

glass

hammer

Draw a line under the right word or fill in the blank.

1. It is **a tool used for pounding.**   slam   library   **hammer**

2. It means **to make bigger.**   magnify   large   great

3. It means **taking shape.**   magnifying   forming   glass

4. It is **a small, round stone.**   earth   hill   pebble

5. It is **a place where books are kept for everyone to use.**
   form   store   library

6. Write the word that is made from **magnify.**

   _____

H-8   Stories without Words

Did you know that much of the earth is made of rock? Everywhere about you, there are rocks. Rocks make hills, and rocks make mountains. Broken rocks make the pebbles beside roads and rivers.

Since long, long ago, rocks have been forming in different ways. Every rock you look at tells a story of something that has happened to the earth.

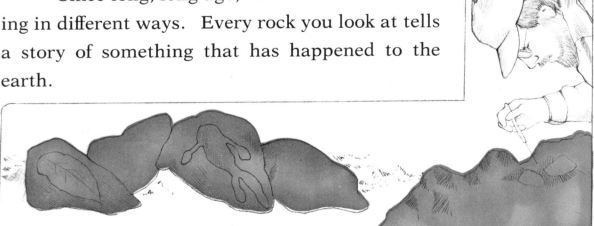

You can have fun collecting rocks for a hobby. Pick up small rocks from different places. Then, get a book about rocks at the library. The book will tell you something about the kinds of rocks you have. A magnifying glass will help you see interesting little things about your rocks. A hammer will help you break them open. Many rocks that are dull on the outside are beautiful inside.

H-8 Testing Yourself

1. Much of the earth we live on is made of _____.

   Draw a line under the right answer.

2. From the story you can tell that
     a. it is difficult to find samples for a rock collection.
     b. it makes the hobby more interesting to know what kinds of rocks you have collected.
     c. you should have only one kind of rock in your collection.

3. The story as a whole is about
     a. cliffs and mountains.   c. telling stories.
     b. using a hammer.   d. rock collecting.

4. All rocks are formed in the same way.   Yes   No   Does not say

5. The inside of a rock always looks like the outside.

                                      Yes   No   Does not say

6. What word in line ten of the story means **bringing together?**

   _____

143

Keeping Track of the Number Right

1. The first chart can be filled in after each test. In the first square, write the total right for the first test in Unit A.

A perfect total score for Unit A would be 48. The total possible for all tests would be 384.

	Units								
Tests	A	B	C	D	E	F	G	H	
1									
2									
3									
4									
5									
6									
7									
8									Total
Total									

2. To begin the second chart, look back over the test pages for Unit **A.** Count the number of times Question 1 was answered right. Put that number in the first square. Continue for each question in each unit.

These figures tell you what you need to know to fill in the graphs on the next page.

A perfect score for all tests in each unit would be 48.

Units

Questions	A	B	C	D	E	F	G	H	Total
1									
2									
3									
4									
5									
6									
Total									

Keeping Track of Growth

Study this sample graph. To record the score for Unit A, put a dot on the line beside the number which tells how often Question 4 was answered right. Do the same for Units B, C, and so on. Draw a line to join the dots. The line will show how this reading skill is growing.

Notice that each graph records the progress made on one question. See how this reader improved in answering Question 4 in each unit except Unit E.

Diagnostic Progress Records

Sample

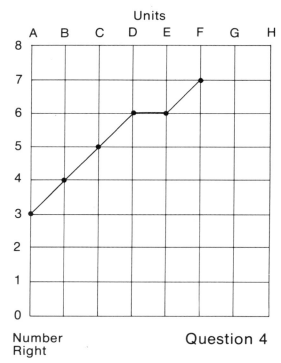

Number Right   Question 4

Giving Direct Details

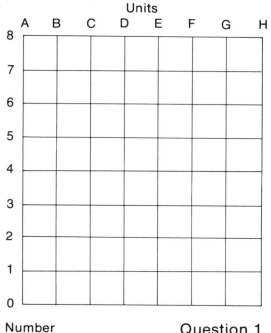

Units

Number Right

Question 1

Giving Implied Details

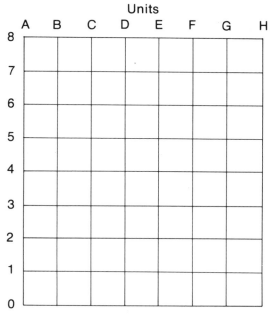

Units

Number Right

Question 2

Seeing the Meaning of the Whole

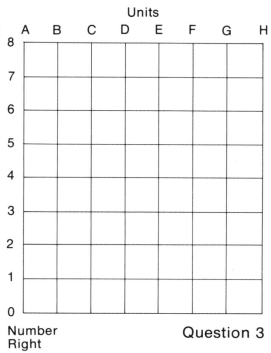

Units

Number Right

Question 3

Checking on Ideas

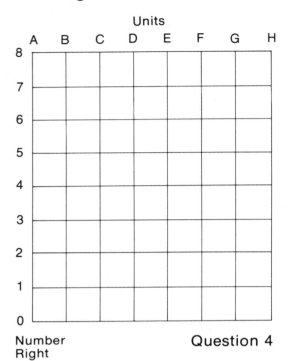

Units

Question 4

Number Right

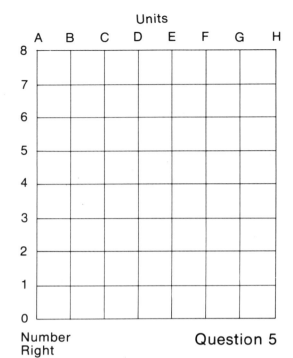

Units

Question 5

Number Right

Understanding Words

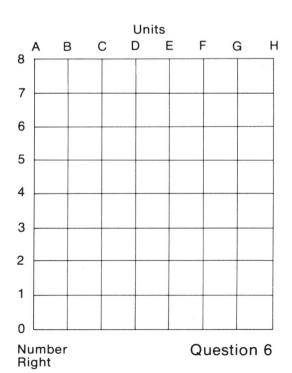

Units

Question 6

Number Right

148